James Frith Jeffers

History Of Canada

James Frith Jeffers

History Of Canada

ISBN/EAN: 9783743328143

Manufactured in Europe, USA, Canada, Australia, Japa

Cover: Foto ©ninafisch / pixelio.de

Manufactured and distributed by brebook publishing software (www.brebook.com)

James Frith Jeffers

History Of Canada

History Primers.

HISTORY OF CANADA.

BY

J. FRITH JEFFERS, M.A.

New and Enlarged Edition.

TORONTO:
CANADA PUBLISHING COMPANY.
1894.

Entered according to the Act of Parliament of Canada in the year one thousand eight hundred and ninety-four, by CANADA PUBLISHING COMPANY (Limited), in the office of the Minister of Agriculture.

PREFACE

The first edition of this Primer of the History of Canada was published in 1878. In 1884, at the instance of the Minister of Education for Ontario, it was revised and the narrative brought down to that date. From the first, it has been in more or less general use in our Canadian schools, and the writer begs to acknowledge the kindness, with which it has been received by teachers and pupils.

In the present edition, the little book has again been carefully revised, and its story continued to 1894. The "questions for written tests," given in former editions, are omitted in this, and there is added instead, a table of **Leading Facts** arranged, not as a mere "list of dates," but according to *periods* and their *features*, for assistance in *reviews*, for reference in *comparative reading*, and, as an aid to the pupils in preparing their *written exercises* upon themes assigned to them.

The words in heavy type are for use in the **oral drill** of classes. Such words indicate the topics, about which teacher and pupils may question each other to the fullest extent.

No maps have been added to the book, lest their insertion should prevent a diligent reference to the correct and complete atlases now in use in all Canadian schools. It is urged, however, that these be consulted for the location of the events of the history.

The teacher will readily perceive the purpose of the writer, in the pages relating the events of the past ten years, namely, to suggest attention, to the *manner of development* of "public questions" in the history of the Dominion.

It may be safely affirmed, that the public interest—even that of our young people—has been more attracted to the progress of these questions, than to the individuality of the statesmen engaged in the promotion of the issues involved.

J. F. J.

TORONTO, 1894.

LEADING FACTS

IN THE

HISTORY OF CANADA.

Periods, and their Special Features.	A.D.	EVENTS.
Discovery and Exploration.	1492	**Columbus** (for Spain) discovers the Bahama Islands.
	1497	John Cabot (for England) discovers Newfoundland.
	1498	Sebastian Cabot (for England) explores the Atlantic coast from Labrador to Florida.
	1534-35	**Jacques Cartier** (for France) explores the St. Lawrence Gulf and River, and takes possession of the country.

CANADA UNDER FRANCE.

☞ Events of English interference are printed in italics.

Settlement and Government by means of Trading Companies— 1541 to 1663.	1541	Roberval is given a *Trading Monopoly* and made first Viceroy of Canada. He and the settlers embarked with him lost at sea.
	1583	*Sir Humphrey Gilbert (for England) takes possession of Newfoundland.*
	1598	Marquis de la Roche receives the renewal of Roberval's *Monopoly*. His expedition a failure.
	1599	A settlement of sixteen persons made at *Tadoussac*, by merchants acting under the same patent of monopoly.

CANADA UNDER FRANCE.—Continued.

PERIODS, AND THEIR SPECIAL FEATURES.	A.D.	EVENTS.
	1605	Port Royal (Annapolis), in Acadia, founded by De Monts.
	1608	**Quebec** founded by **Champlain**, an officer of the "Fur Company."
	1610	Henry Hudson explores Hudson Bay.
	1622	Sir George Calvert (Lord Baltimore) plants the first English colony in Newfoundland.
	1624	Acadia granted to Sir Wm. Alexander, by whom it is named *Nova Scotia*.
	1627	Cardinal Richelieu forms the Company of "*One Hundred Associates*," but war with England prevents its acting under its charter. Canada named *New France*. Champlain made Governor.
	1628	The English capture the ships of the "Company" and take Acadia.
	1629	The English take Quebec.
	1632	The *Treaty of St. Germain-en-Laye* restores Canada to France, and the new trading company enters upon its duties.
	1635	Death of Champlain at Quebec.
Indian Wars— 1637 to 1667.	1642	*Montreal* founded under the name of Marianapolis.
	1654	Sir David Kirke founds a second English colony in Newfoundland. New Englanders take Acadia.
	1663	Bishop Laval founds the Quebec Seminary, afterwards Laval University.
Canada made a Crown-Colony of France— 1663 to 1760.	1663	The rule of "Fur Companies" ended. The Province taken under "**Royal Government**." Introduction of French law (Coutume de Paris).
	1667	The *Treaty of Breda* restores Acadia to France. (Chap. xv.)
	1670	Charles II. grants "Hudson Bay Company" a charter for two hundred years.
	1672	*Cataraqui* (Kingston) made a permanent fort.

CANADA UNDER FRANCE.—*Continued.*

Periods, and their Special Features.	A.D.	Events.
	1673	Father Marquette and Joliette reach the head waters of the Mississippi.
	1681, '82	La Salle explores the river to the Gulf of Mexico, and names the country passed *Louisiana*.
Colonial Wars— New France against New England— 1689 to 1759.	1689	The French raid New England colonies.
	1690	The English colonies plan two expeditions against New France and take Port Royal.
	1696	France gets control of Newfoundland.
	1697	The *Treaty of Ryswick* ends the war.
	1701	The French found *Detroit*.
	1703	"Queen Anne's War" breaks out and lasts ten years. The French gain Newfoundland and lose Acadia.
	1713	The *Treaty of Utrecht* gives to England Acadia, Newfoundland, and Hudson Bay Territory, and cedes the Islands of Miquelon and St. Pierre to France.
	1731	Montreal merchants explore the North-West and found Fort Maurepas (Winnipeg).
	1745	France loses the Islands of Cape Breton and St. John (Prince Edward).
	1747	Fort Rouillé (Toronto) built.
	1748	The *Treaty of Aix-la-Chapelle* restores the Islands of Cape Breton and St. John to France.
	1749	*Halifax* founded by the English.
	1755	General Braddock defeated in the Ohio Valley. The English remove the Acadians from Nova Scotia and disperse them among their Atlantic colonies.
	1756	General Montcalm takes command of French troops in New France.
	1758	The English take Louisbourg and grant a Constitution and *Elective Assembly* to Nova Scotia.
	1759	The English take *Quebec*.

CANADA UNDER GREAT BRITAIN.

Periods, and their Special Features.	A.D.	Events.
Military Occupation—1760 to 1763.	1760	Canada surrendered to General Amherst.
	1763	The **Treaty of Paris** gives to England the possessions of France in North America, except the Islands of Miquelon and St. Pierre.
Canada a Crown Colony of England—1763 to 1791.	1770	Prince Edward Island made a separate province.
	1773	Prince Edward Island receives a constitution.
"Quebec Act"—1774.	1774	**Quebec Act** extends Canada's boundaries from Hudson Bay to Ohio Valley, within which French civil law and English criminal law are established.
	1775	The thirteen Atlantic colonies revolt from England, invade Canada, and take Montreal.
	1776	The invaders are driven out of Canada.
	1783	The *Treaty of Versailles* acknowledges the independence of the thirteen colonies, which become the United States.
	1784	*United Empire Loyalists* move from the States into Nova Scotia, New Brunswick and west of the River Ottawa.
	1784	New Brunswick made a separate province.
"Constitutional Act"—1791 to 1841.	1791	**Constitutional Act** divides Canada into two provinces, each with a governor and parliament, and authorizes the forming of the *Clergy Reserves*.
	1792	Captain Vancouver explores the Pacific coast.
	1792	**Upper Canada** opens its first Parliament at Newark (Niagara), 17th of September, and that of **Lower Canada** meets at Quebec, 17th of December.
	1793	Slavery abolished in Upper Canada.
	1794	Town of *York* (Toronto) founded by Governor Simcoe.
	1795	The Upper Canada Parliament meets at York.
	1803	Slavery abolished in Lower Canada.

CANADA UNDER GREAT BRITAIN.—*Continued.*

Periods, and their Special Features.	A.D.	Events.
	1803	Lord Selkirk promotes the settlement of Prince Edward Island.
	1804-17	New Brunswick governed by Presidents.
	1809	Great Britain makes a *timber duty* in favor of New Brunswick.
	1811	Lord Selkirk founds a settlement at Red River.
War 1812 to 1814. (Chap. X.)	1812	United States invade Canada.
	1814	The *Treaty of Ghent*, December 14th, restores peace.
	1816	Schools established in Upper Canada.
Political Agitation —1817 to 1837.	1817	First banks—Montreal and Quebec—opened in Canada.
	1817	Agitation against the *Clergy Reserves*.
	1819	Welland Canal projected by Hon. W. H. Merritt.
	1821	Lachine Canal commenced.
	1823	*Canada Trade Act* regulates duties between Upper and Lower Canada.
	1832-34	Cholera.
	1834	York made a city under the name of *Toronto*. W. Lyon Mackenzie the first Mayor.
	1837, 38	Canadian Rebellion.
	1838	**Lord Durham** investigates the troubles in Canada, and recommends a union of the provinces.
	1839	Courts-martial.
	1840	**Union Bill** passed by the British Parliament, July 23rd.
	1841	*Union Bill* goes into operation, February 10th.
Legislative Union of the two Canadas—1841 to 1867.	1841	First Union Parliament meets at *Kingston*, June 13th.
	1841	Present municipal system established.
	1842	**Ashburton Treaty** defines the boundary line between Canada and United States, and provides for extradition of criminals.

CANADA UNDER GREAT BRITAIN. —Continued.

Periods, and their Special Features.	A.D.	Events.
	1843	Hudson Bay Company founds **Victoria**, Vancouver Island.
	1844	Seat of Government changed from Kingston to Montreal.
	1844-47	Rev. Dr. Ryerson inaugurates the present **system** of *schools* in Upper Canada.
	1846-'51	Separate Schools established.
Responsible Government.	1847	Lord Elgin, Governor-General.
	1847	*Duties* in favor of British manufactures *abolished* by Home Government.
	1848	St. Lawrence *canals* completed.
	1849	*Rebellion Losses Bill* passed. Riots in Montreal. Seat of Government changed to meet alternately at Toronto and Quebec.
	1851	British Government transfers the **Post-office** department to the Canadian Government. Rate of postage made uniform. *Postage stamps* used.
	1851	First World's Exhibition at London, England.
	1851	Responsible Government given to Prince Edward Island.
	1852	*Municipal Loan Fund Act.*
	1854	*Reciprocity Treaty* with the United States.
	1854	*Seigniorial Tenure Act.*
Period of Reforms.	1854	*Clergy Reserves Act.*
	1855	Responsible Government granted to Newfoundland.
	1856	Legislative Council of Canada made elective.
Material Progress.	1856	Grand Trunk Railway completed between Toronto and Montreal.
	1858	Decimal currency adopted in Canada.
	1858	Her Majesty selects **Ottawa** to be the permanent seat of Government.
	1858	*Atlantic Cable* laid between Ireland and Newfoundland.
	1859	*British Columbia* constituted a province.

HISTORY OF CANADA.   13

CANADA UNDER GREAT BRITAIN.—*Continued.*

Periods, and their Special Features.	A.D.	EVENTS.
Confederation discussions.	1860	The **Prince of Wales** visits Canada, opens the Victoria Bridge at Montreal, and lays the corner-stone of the new Parliament buildings at Ottawa.
	1861-65	American *Civil War.* "Trent" Affair. Raids.
	1864	*Convention* of Provincial Delegates meets at Quebec and passes seventy-two resolutions in favor of *Confederation* of the provinces.
	1865	The resolutions adopted by the Canadas, Nova Scotia and New Brunswick.
	1866	Fenian Raids.
	1866	*Reciprocity Treaty* terminates.
	1866	First meeting of Parliament at *Ottawa*, the new capital, June 8th.
Dominion of Canada—1867.	1867	The **British North America Act** brought before the British Parliament, February 7th.
	1867	*Dominion Day,* July 1st. The first Parliament of the Dominion meets, November 6th.
	1868	*Rupert's Land Act* transfers Hudson Bay Territory to the Dominion.
	1869	Red River Rebellion.
	1870	**Manitoba** constituted a province of the Dominion.
	1871	**British Columbia** joins the Dominion.
	1871	New Brunswick abolishes Separate schools.
	1871	**Washington Treaty** passed.
	1872	Arbitration gives the Island of San Juan to the United States.
	1872	*Dual Representation* abolished.
	1873	**Municipal Relief Fund Bill** passed in Ontario.
	1873	**Prince Edward Island** joins the Dominion.

CANADA UNDER GREAT BRITAIN.—*Continued.*

Periods, and their Special Features.	A.D.	EVENTS.
Inter-Provincial relations.	1873	Pacific Railway Scandal. The Government of Sir John Macdonald resigns, and is succeeded by that of Hon. Alex. Mackenzie.
	1874	The **Ballot Act** passed.
	1875	Ontario—the Department of Education made a department of Government—Hon. Adam Crooks first Minister of Education.
	1876	Inter-Colonial Railway completed.
	1878	*Halifax Commission* settles fishery claims under the Washington Treaty.
	1879	Sir John Macdonald returns to power upon the question of a **Protective Tariff**.
	1880	Office of *High Commissioner* to Great Britain created—Sir A. T. Galt first High Commissioner.
	1882	North-West Territories divided into four Districts. **Regina** made the capital.
	1882	Redistribution Bill.
	1884	Canadian volunteers in *Egypt*.
	1885	North-West Rebellion.
	1885	Dominion **Franchise Act** passed.
	1885	Canadian Pacific Railway completed to the Pacific coast.
	1885	*Fishery clauses* of the Washington Treaty terminate.
	1886	*Chinese* Immigration Act.
	1886	Colonial and Indian Exhibition at London, England.
	1887	**Jubilee Year** of Her Majesty's reign.
	1888	Order of the Jesuits incorporated in the Province of Quebec.
International relations.	1888	Jesuits' Estates Bill passed.
	1890	Separate schools abolished in Manitoba.
	1890	Canadian **sealing vessels** in the North Pacific seized by United States cruisers.
	1891	Death of Sir John Macdonald.

CANADA UNDER GREAT BRITAIN.—*Continued.*

Periods, and their Special Features.	A.D.	EVENTS.
	1891	Sir J. J. C. Abbott, Premier.
	1891	Jamaica Exposition.
	1891	First Canadian Pacific steamship from **Japan** arrives at **Vancouver**, April 29th.
	1891	Grand Trunk Railway opens its **St. Clair Tunnel** for traffic, September 19th.
	1891	Legislative Council abolished in New Brunswick.
	1892	Death of Hon. Alex. Mackenzie.
	1892	One hundredth anniversary of **Upper Canada** (Ontario) Parliament.
	1892	Two hundred and fiftieth anniversary of the founding of **Montreal**.
	1892	Sir John Thompson, Premier of the Dominion.
	1893	Court of Arbitration at Paris settles **Behring Sea Sealing** question.
Inter-Colonial relations.	1894	*Commercial Treaty* with *France* ratified.
	1894	**Inter-Colonial Conference** at Ottawa.

■

HISTORY OF CANADA.

CHAPTER I.
INTRODUCTION—DISCOVERIES.

1. Sister studies.
2. The History of Canada.
3. America four hundred years ago.
4. America now.
5, 6. What led to the settlement of America.
7. Trade four hundred years ago.
8. Columbus.
9. Spaniards.
10. England—Cabot.
11. France—Newfoundland.
12. Cartier.
13. Roberval.

1. If we wish to know everything about a country, we must study both its Geography and History ; hence these have been called **sister studies,** and they should be carried on at the same time. The former names the limits of the country, traces its rivers, measures the height of its mountains, or describes the number and position of its cities ; the latter relates to all that is known about the people who have ever lived in it, their condition when they first settled there, and what they have since done to make themselves either better or worse. If the nation has waged any wars we learn their causes and what resulted from them, what happened in times of peace, how the country has been governed, and through what changes the government may have passed ; while, mingled with the story, we shall read the names of the men who have had anything to do with making the name of their country an honor.

2. **The History of Canada** describes the condition of this country when people first came hither from Europe, relates how the Province of Quebec came to be settled by the French, and the other provinces by the English. It explains why the United States, where the English language is spoken, are not under the same government as Canada, and tells why Canadians call England the Mother Country. It also tells us how each province began and grew in numbers, extent, and wealth ; and how they all came afterwards to form the Union called the **Dominion of Canada.** In it we read the names of such men as Cartier and Champlain,

Wolfe and Montcalm, Brock and Tecumseh, and many others, who have done much to build up and advance Canada.

3. Take the map of the world and note well the position of Europe to the east, and of America to the west, of the Atlantic Ocean. Four hundred years ago the people of Europe knew nothing about America. No ship had then been know to sail directly across that wide water; no city of New York, or Halifax, or Quebec existed then, but great forests grew where these cities now are. The only people living at that time in this part of the continent were Indians, who built no houses, but dwelt in tents or huts, made of bark or skins, and called wigwams. They had no roads, but travelled, hunted, or fought their battles through the woods that shaded all the land; while long journeys were made upon the rivers and lakes in bark or wooden canoes. They had no books, and knew very little of the Creator, whom they called the Great Spirit. They were bold and cunning, generous to their friends, but bitterly revengeful to their foes. There were, however, some great chiefs among them, who were noted for their love of the people, their honesty, and their kindness to enemies.

4. How different is America now, studded with cities, towns and villages, crossed by roads and railways, while steamboats and vessels go to and fro upon its large lakes and rivers! Much of the forest has been cleared away, and in its place fields of grain wave in the sunlight, and churches, schools, and farm-houses dot the surface of the country. You seldom see an Indian now, and the most of the people in America have light complexions like the people in Europe. The reason is, they are either Europeans, or the descendants of Europeans.

5. How have these changes happened? What led the people of Europe to find their way across the ocean—across three thousand miles of water—to this continent? And when they found it covered with forests and inhabited by savages, why did they come back to it again, more and more of them, until the whole land is now in the possession of the white man?

6. If you look around you thoughtfully, you will learn the very cause that led to the settlement of America. You will see that the people do not spend their time in hunting and fishing, as the Indians did, but in tilling the ground, in buying and selling, and

INTRODUCTION—DISCOVERIES. 19

sending their grain and merchandize to other lands, for which they bring back goods not produced in this country. It was this **desire to trade,** which led the white man across the Atlantic.

7. Look next at the map of the Eastern Hemisphere. Four hundred years ago the European nations that were great traders were the English, French, Spaniards, and some others bordering on the Mediterranean sea. Ships used to sail as far eastward on this sea as Constantinople and other ports, and were there laden with rich goods brought overland from various parts of Asia. A large portion of these goods consisted of spices, beautiful cloths, gems and precious stones, and gold and silver from **India.** In this way Europeans heard of that distant land, and many were the fables related of its rich mines, its people, fruits, and animals. Merchants wished to reach it, and travellers who had been there and to China, came back and told that there was a great sea to the east of Asia, like that to the west of Europe. As time went on, the strife in trade increased, and Spain and Portugal became the greatest of commercial nations. Brave mariners ventured to sail down the coast of Africa, and the Portuguese had small settlements here and there, as far as the Cape of Good Hope, but their ships were yet too frail to weather its storms, and their courage was not bold enough to lead them around it.

8. All these years learned men, merchants, and sailors were thinking of the Atlantic Ocean, and wondering whither a voyage westward on its waters would lead them. Some thought, and among them **Christopher Columbus,** a brave sailor from Genoa in Italy, that it must be the same sea that washed the east coast of China, and that by it they might find a shorter way to the famous India. This great man was the first to believe that land would be reached by sailing westward, and spent several years in trying to persuade the monarchs of different countries to furnish him with ships to prove its existence. But none were willing to venture their ships and men, until, in A.D. 1492, Queen Isabella, of Spain, by pledging her jewels, fitted out three small vessels, and gave the command of them to Columbus. In August of that year he set out from Palos, in Spain, and on the 12th of October, landed on San Salvador, one of the islands of the Bahama group. After exploring many of the islands now called the West

Indies, he returned to Europe, taking with him specimens of gold and fruits, also several of the natives, whom he called **Indians**, for he thought he had landed on islands near the eastern coast of the fabled India of Asia, which he had set out to find.

9. There was great surprise when Columbus returned, for no person in Spain expected to see him or his companions again. But when nobles and merchants heard of the beautiful islands he had found, of the strange people he had seen, and above all of the gold to be had across the Atlantic, surprise gave way to eagerness to go there themselves, and it was not many years before the Spaniards had spread over much of South and Central America. In these regions were **rich mines** of gold and silver, which led that nation to claim possession of them. In the more northern parts they did not discover the precious metals, so were not anxious to settle the country, and thus all of it north of Mexico and Florida was left to be explored by other nations of Europe.

10. Of these, **England** was the first to explore the coasts of America. In 1497, King Henry VII. sent out **John Cabot**, a merchant of Bristol, to make discoveries. This man arrived off the coast of Newfoundland, which he was the first to see. In the next year his son, **Sebastian**, visited all the coast from Labrador to Florida, and claimed it in the name of England. But England was then disturbed by civil war, arising out of the rebellion of Perkin Warbeck, and was not able to follow up the advantage of her prior discoveries in the region about the St. Lawrence, and thus lost her chance of peaceably possessing what she afterwards acquired by conquest.

11. **France** was the nation which ranked next in projects of discovery. As early as 1506, French vessels came to the banks of Newfoundland for the purpose of fishing for the cod and whale, which were highly prized in Europe. They also tried to settle the adjoining coasts, but these attempts did not succeed, for the stories of golden treasures, found by the Spaniards farther to the southward, made the French restless to acquire like riches. Moreover, the old thought of reaching India by a short route westward still possessed the minds of men in Europe.

12. It was this thought which influenced **Jacques Cartier**, in 1534 and '5, to explore the St. Lawrence Gulf and River, to

which he gave their names. He went up the river as far as Hochelaga, where Montreal now stands, and gave to the chief rivers and islands he passed the names they now bear. The word Montreal is derived from the French name Mont (English, Mount) Royal, which he bestowed upon the mountain standing behind the present city; while the name **Canada** became applied to the whole country, because he often heard the natives use it, although it meant simply a village.

13. In 1541, the King of France made the Lord of Roberval the **first viceroy** of Canada. Roberval and Cartier made several voyages to the St. Lawrence, touching at Newfoundland, and exploring the neighboring islands and coasts. The last voyage was in 1549, when Roberval set sail from France, taking with him a large number of people, in order to form a settlement; but they were all lost at sea, and this disaster so discouraged the king, that for nearly fifty years no effort was made to colonize Canada. Cartier, in one of his voyages, had left a small settlement at a place a little above where Quebec now stands, but it dwindled away. The people were not used to the circumstances of a new country, and did not know how to support themselves, so that many died from disease, and the remainder went back to France.

CHAPTER II.

SETTLEMENT OF CANADA BY THE FRENCH.

1. English voyages—Frobisher—Gilbert—Drake.
2, 3. Fisheries—Fur trade.
4. De la Roche.
5. Pontgravé and Chauvin.
6. Champlain.
7. Quebec founded.
8. Champlain's explorations.
9, 10, 11. Champlain's difficulties.
12. The "One Hundred Associates."
13. Treaty of St. Germain-en-Laye.
14. Death of Champlain.

1. About the time that France relaxed her efforts, England began once more to take an interest in the New World. The latter nation laid claim to the whole of the coast-line from Labrador to Florida, because she had been the first to visit it in 1497. The voyages of the French aroused the jealousy of the English, so that this feeling between the two countries became one means of keeping their attention directed to this continent.

In 1575, the English, under **Martin Frobisher**, arrived at Newfoundland, and in 1583, **Sir Humphrey Gilbert** took possession of the island in the name of Queen Elizabeth. **Sir Francis Drake** visited it in 1585.

2. Although, for nearly fifty years after the death of Roberval, the court of France sent out no expedition to the St. Lawrence, the vessels of private merchants came regularly every year to Newfoundland to fish, and the French began to trade with the Indians for furs or pelts. The wild animals, from which the furs were taken, were very abundant in the forests of America, and the Indians very skilled in the pursuit of them. In exchange for these pelts, the traders gave beads, trinkets, colored cloth, or other cheap goods, and afterwards sold the furs in France at good prices, often making thereby large fortunes. Thus, two sources of rich traffic opened to the French in America, namely, the **fisheries** of Newfoundland and the **fur trade**, which, if wisely used, would have done more good for France, than the gold and silver mines of the south did for Spain.

3. Several sea-port towns of France, **Dieppe, Rochelle, Rouen**, and **St. Malo,** became rivals in sending out ships and men to engage in the fur trade. They tried to get the advantage of one another, and each sought to persuade the king to give it the sole right to carry on this trade, promising, as a return for such a favor, to carry out settlers, and to do other things for the public good. It was the custom, in those days, for kings to hold the power to grant leave to certain persons to pursue a special trade, and for this privilege, or **monopoly**, the merchant so favored had to pay the king a fixed sum of money or do some service for the state. If he could not perform his promise, the king would take away the privileges he had granted, and give them to someone else.

4. The French king, Henry IV., thought he might secure all the benefits of the fur trade for himself, and in 1598 appointed the **Marquis de la Roche**, viceroy of Canada and Acadia,* giving him all the power that Roberval had formerly held, and instructed him to break up the traffic which the merchants had

---

*The country lying about the Bay of Fundy, now called Nova Scotia and New Brunswick.

carried on. But just as De la Roche neared the coast of Acadia, a storm arose, which drove him back to France, and made a failure of his expedition.

5. In the meantime, a merchant of St. Malo, named **Pontgravé**, and a master sailor of Rouen, named **Chauvin**, joining together in 1599, secured the privileges bestowed upon the viceroy, and promised to settle a colony of five hundred persons in Canada, the king granting them a **monopoly** of the fur trade in return. The title of Lieutenant-General was given to Chauvin. During four years they made three voyages, and carried to France large cargoes of furs. But they brought out only sixteen settlers, who were left at **Tadoussac**, where they would have died from starvation, had not the Indians in kindness supplied their wants.

6. Chauvin died in 1603, and **De Chastes**, the Governor of Dieppe, was the next Lieutenant-General of Canada. He persuaded the merchants of the several towns already named to form a Company for purposes of trade. Three vessels were fitted out, and the command of them was given to a young naval officer, **Samuel de Champlain**. This officer, while promoting the "fur trade," which was one of the objects of the expedition, valued it chiefly as a means of attracting settlers to Canada. He busied himself in travelling through the forests, and along the rivers of the new country, in order to learn all about it. He was a pious man, and of a generous disposition. thinking only of the good of the people. He spent thirty-two years in forming the colony on the St. Lawrence, and was in fact the founder of the Province of Quebec.

7. In his first voyage, 1603, he ascended the St. Lawrence as far as the rapids above Montreal, and, because of the prevalent hope of reaching Asia by a short water route across this continent, he called these rapids **Lachine**, from the French words—*à la Chine*—to China. When he returned to France, his report of the country excited a greater interest with regard to Canada, than had ever been felt before. But De Chastes had died while Champlain was in Canada, and was succeeded by **De Monts**, who selected **Acadia** for settlement, in preference to Canada. A small colony was founded in 1605, at a place on the Bay of Fundy, called at

the time Port Royal, but now **Annapolis**. Champlain, however, advocated the claims of Canada, as the country along the St. Lawrence was called, and obtained two vessels with which to proceed there. He did so, and on the 3rd of July, 1608, laid the foundation of the present city of **Quebec**, by erecting a few rude buildings of wood for dwellings, and a wooden fort, whither the settlers might go in times of danger. In 1611, he named the present site of Montreal, Place Royale, and the island in front of it, St. Helen, after his wife.

8. Champlain was the first white man who made a journey farther west than Lachine. In 1615, he went up the **Ottawa**, and reached the lakes **Nipissing** and **Huron**, and then passed down to Lake **Ontario**. In this year missionaries of the Catholic Church came out from France, and by their zeal and diligence, not only kept the settlements together, but also persuaded large numbers of the Indians to profess the Christian religion, and live somewhat as white people do.

9. Champlain must have been very persevering, or he would have given up the work of settling Canada, on account of the many difficulties. Shortly after the founding of Quebec he made an error, by mixing himself and the French in the wars which the Indians were constantly carrying on among themselves. At this time there were two large tribes of Indians living north of the St. Lawrence, in the country through which Champlain had travelled. These tribes were the **Algonquins** and **Hurons**. To the south of the river, in what is now the State of New York, lived the **Iroquois** nation, made up of several smaller tribes, from which they afterwards took their name of the Six Nations. The Algonquins and Hurons were always at war with the Iroquois, and asked Champlain to help them. He thought by doing so he would make the Algonquins friends of the French, who could thus live more safely in the country. But it proved otherwise, for the Iroquois were very powerful, so that the Algonquins were beaten, and, after a time, looked to the French to protect them instead of being a safeguard to the young colony.

10. Another source of trouble to Champlain was the constant change of governors. In 1612, De Monts gave place to the Count de Soissons, who died the same year, and was followed by his

brother, the Prince de Condé. In 1616, Condé sold his office to the Admiral de Montmorency for 11,000 crowns, a fact which shows Canada was beginning to be valued. Montmorency became dissatisfied with the trouble his office gave him, and, in 1624, handed it over to his nephew, the Duke de Ventadour. These governors lived in France, and never came to Canada, but each one in succession made Champlain his **Deputy-Governor**. All these changes disturbed his plans, and obliged him to spend much time in going to France, in order to maintain an interest in the colony, which grew very slowly, the settlement of Quebec having only sixty inhabitants in the year 1620.

11. The "**Company of Merchants**" was a third great cause of much anxiety to the Deputy-Governor. According to their charter, the company should have supplied the settlers with all that was necessary for a young colony, until the people could support themselves. But the merchants thought only of the profits of the fur trade, and the colonists, not being able to clear the land and raise food for themselves, engaged in hunting, and thus had to depend upon the ships of the company for their chief support. Champlain had to complain so often of the bad faith of the merchants, that at length their charter was taken from them, and given to two gentlemen named De Caën, in 1621; but these only made matters worse, and six years afterwards things were altogether changed.

12. At this time Cardinal Richelieu was the Prime Minister of France. He undertook, in 1627, to help Canada, by forming another and a stronger protection for it, called the "**Company of One Hundred Associates.**" In their charter, the new company promised to send out three hundred tradesmen to New France, and to furnish all those who settled in the country with all necessary tools, and food for three years, after which each person was to be allowed sufficient land, and grain for seed. They also engaged to have 6,000 French settled in the country before the year 1643, and to establish three priests in each settlement. The latter were to be maintained for fifteen years, after which they were to receive cleared lands, for the support of the "Catholic Church in New France." In return for these services, the king gave the company all the rights of the fur trade, and of all the

commerce with the settlements along the sea-coast and the River St. Lawrence, but withheld the whale and cod fisheries. He also gave them two ships of war, and—what was more important than anything else—granted the company the ownership of all the land and forts in Canada, Acadia, and Cape Breton. In the charter these provinces received the name of **New France** (Nouvelle France). Champlain was made Governor, and the office of viceroy was done away with, after having lasted eighty-six years, from 1541 to 1627.

13. Just at this time, however, war broke out between France and England, and in 1628 the English, under Sir David Kirke, captured the first ships laden with stores sent out by the company. The next year, 1629, the **English took** Quebec, and remained masters of Canada until 1632, when by the treaty of **St. Germain-en-Laye**, Canada, Acadia, and Cape Breton were given back to France.

14. The next year, Champlain came again to Quebec with plenty of stores, and some more settlers. He now became very busy arranging the affairs of the colony, and trying to keep peace among the Indians. But Christmas Day of 1635 was a very sad one in Canada, for on that day Champlain died, and the country lost its best friend. In the same year the first Canadian College was opened at Quebec.

CHAPTER III.

ENGLISH COLONIES—INDIAN WARS—EXPLORATIONS

1, 2, 3. English and French colonies compared.
4. Montreal founded.
5. Missionaries.
6, 7. Indian wars.
8. Earthquakes.
9. Royal Government.
10. Marquis de Tracy.
11. Cataraqui (Kingston) founded.
12. Marquette—Joliette—La Salle.
13. Liquor traffic.

1. At the time of Champlain's death, the French population in Canada consisted of several small settlements, extending from Tadoussac to Lachine, the most important of which were at Quebec and Three Rivers. In Acadia, which included the Provinces now called New Brunswick and Nova Scotia, there were

only a few forts, or trading-posts, along the coast or at the mouths of rivers.

2. Take a map of North America, and while reading the following list of dates, find the places mentioned.

Virginia, founded by Sir Walter Raleigh, 1607.
New York, founded by the Dutch, 1609.
Massachusetts, settled by the "Pilgrim Fathers," 1620.
New Hampshire, settled by the English, 1623.
Maine, settled by the English, 1625.
New Jersey and **Delaware,** settled by the Dutch and Swedes, 1627.
Rhode Island, settled from Massachusetts, 1631.
Maryland, settled by the English under Lord Baltimore, 1634.
Connecticut, settled from Massachusetts, 1635.

3. The English had again turned their attention to America, and, in the short space of thirty years, had done more in forming settlements than the French did in all the time since Cartier sailed up the St. Lawrence. It is necessary to keep these facts in mind, for in Europe, France and England were often at war, and the strife was then kept up between the French on the St. Lawrence, and the English along the Atlantic. Again, the English made friends with the Iroquois, and bought furs from them, in the same way that the French dealt with the Algonquins and Hurons. The English devoted themselves to cutting down the forests, and tilling the land, the same as they do to-day; while the French liked better to hunt, and engage in the fur trade, thus neglecting their farms. The result was, that the English colonies grew faster, and supported themselves; but the French had to depend very much upon supplies from France.

4. **De Montmagny** succeeded Champlain, and arrived at Quebec in 1637. He found that he would have much trouble in protecting the interests of his colony. The Iroquois had obtained fire-arms from the English and Dutch, and for several years there was an **Indian war,** until peace was made in 1642. In this year the settlement on the Island of Montreal was increased, and received the name of the city of Mary, or Marianapolis, but we will speak of it as **Montreal.** From this time it began to be a place of importance in the history of the country. The "Com-

pany of One Hundred Associates", now became as lax as the former company, and, in 1647, ceded the fur trade to the inhabitants of Quebec, Montreal, and Three Rivers, for one thousand beaver skins a year.

5. The following year **D'Ailleboust** became Governor. He was very diligent in his duties, and Canada became more prosperous. The priests, who came out as missionaries, did very much for the people, and the success of the colony at this time was largely due to them. They persuaded the Hurons to live together in villages, and taught them Christianity. They sought to induce other tribes to do the same, and went boldly among the Indians at great distances from the settlements, even among the Iroquois. But nothing could conquer the enmity which this nation had towards the Algonquins, and still more towards the Hurons. The Iroquois said it was a shame for the Hurons to lay aside their Indian habits, and become Christians. They were jealous also of the friendship between the French and Hurons, and were resolved to break it up. This they did in 1648, when they stole quietly along the rivers, and through the woods, into Canada, and fell suddenly upon a Huron village near Lake Simcoe, killing the inhabitants and the missionary, and burning the church and buildings. Then they went away as suddenly as they came. The next year they treated other villages in the same way, so that the poor Hurons, only some three hundred of whom were left, had to find their way to Quebec for protection.

6. The story of Canada, for many years, is largely made up of these **Indian Wars**. The Iroquois became so troublesome that the French were obliged to work with their guns always ready, for they did not know when the Indians might attack them. The tops of trees, the bushes, and even old logs might be a hiding place for some foe. **The Eries,** a tribe that lived on the shores of Lake Erie, were treated even worse than the Hurons, for not one of their number was left.

7. **De Lauson** was made Governor in 1651. He sent to France for three hundred soldiers, but the wars went on, and in 1658, **Viscount d'Argenson** took charge of the colony. He was succeeded, in 1662, by **Baron d'Avaugour.** Four hundred soldiers more were sent to Canada, and increased the strength

of the French so much that the Iroquois left them alone for awhile. This Governor advised the King of France to do away with the "One Hundred Associates," and to take the Province at once under his own care, which was done in 1663. In this year **De Laval**, who was at the head of the Catholic Church in Canada, founded the Quebec Seminary, which has since become the Laval University,

8. There also happened in 1663 a succession of **Earthquakes**, which lasted from February until August. They occurred several times during each day. The first shock was very severe, and was felt throughout the whole extent of Canada. The waving motion of the ground caused the houses to reel backwards and forwards, and large stones to bound hither and thither, while trees were uprooted, giving the forests a swaying motion, which the Indians described by saying, "all the trees were drunk." The ice in the rivers was more than six feet thick, but it was rent and thrown up in large pieces, while from the openings came up clouds of smoke, or fountains of dirt and sand. "Violent as the earthquake was, through the mercy of God, not one life was lost, nor anyone in any way injured.

9. It has been shown that Canada had, for years, been governed by "Fur Companies." In 1663, however, Canada was made a Crown colony, and came directly under **Royal Government**, so that the people became subject to the same laws that prevailed in France, or to what was called the "**Custom of Paris**." **De Mesy** was sent out as Governor, and a council was appointed to assist him. Several of the leading residents of the colony were named members of this council, and were thus led to take deeper interest in its affairs. Courts of law were established at Quebec, Montreal, and Three Rivers. The public officer, next in rank to the Governor, was called the **Intendant**. He was a very important person, for he performed the duties of a minister of finance, police, justice, and public works. He held office as long as his conduct was good, and thus became a great help to the Governors, who were changed very often, and were at first ignorant of what was good for the colony. Indeed the Intendant did the most of the governing, while the Governors, who were military officers, busied themselves in fighting the Indians,

10. The new Governor died before two years passed, and was succeeded in 1665 by the **Marquis de Tracy**, who brought with him a whole regiment, and many new settlers, as well as a supply of sheep, cattle, and horses, now brought into Canada for the first time. This assistance aroused the drooping spirits of the colonists.

11. De Tracy, although seventy years of age, was a very energetic soldier, and resolved to punish the Iroquois at once. He built three forts along the River Richelieu, and, in the middle of winter, waged war against the Indians with such success, that they were glad to make peace with him. In 1667, **De Courcelles** became Governor. He followed up what De Tracy had done, and made haste while peace lasted to make the colony stronger, and to explore the western country. **Talon**, the Intendant, was a wise and good man and helped very much in the work. A new trading-post was made at the Sault Ste. Marie, between Lakes Huron and Superior, and a new fort was begun at **Cataraqui** (Kingston) which was not finished until 1672. About this time the small-pox appeared in Canada, and was very fatal among the Indians.

12. The **Count de Frontenac** was the next ruler, in 1672. He was a great soldier and a very haughty man. He had heard of a great river in the far West, and sent out Father Marquette and a merchant named Joliette to find it. This they did, and came upon the **Mississippi**, in latitude 42° 30'. They followed the course of the river below the mouth of the Arkansas, and then returned to report their discovery. Father Marquette commenced a mission among the Miami Indians at the foot of Lake Michigan, while Joliette was rewarded with a grant of the **Island of Anticosti**. One would think that hereafter we should hear no more of a water route to China across America; but it was not so. Adventurous men still held the notion, and, shortly afterwards, we find a gentleman named **La Salle** asking the Government of France for aid in searching out such a route. Many people still thought it was possible, and La Salle was rewarded, before starting, with the grant of the fort at Cataraqui, and the adjacent land. There went with him a large party, made up of gentlemen, workmen, and pilots. In 1678, he reached Cataraqui, and built a small vessel, the first on Lake Ontario. In this he proceeded as

far as the mouth of the Niagara, and built a small fort there. The next year another vessel called the "Griffon," was set afloat on Lake Erie, and in this La Salle and his party passed up the lake, through Lake **St. Clair**—which he named, and into Lake Michigan. From here the vessel was sent back with a large load of furs, and was never heard of afterwards. La Salle and the rest of his company went on exploring. In 1681, he passed down the Mississippi to the Gulf of Mexico, and claimed possession of all the country along its banks, giving it the name of **Louisiana**, after the name of Louis XIV. king of France. Thus his expedition to China ended.

13. During these ten years Frontenac continued Governor of Canada, but though he seemed desirous of doing great things for the colony, his bad temper led him to quarrel with his Council, the Intendant, and Bishop Laval. The Bishop was much opposed to the traders selling brandy to the Indians, while the Governor took the part of the traders. The King decided against Frontenac, and recalled him to France.

CHAPTER IV.

COLONIAL WARS—CONDITION OF CANADA.

1, 2. Indian troubles.
3. Claims of English and French to New York State.
4. Frontenac.
5. Colonial war—Treaty of Ryswick.
6. Indian Council.
7. Feeling between the Colonies and Canada.
8. Treaty of Utrecht.
9. Condition of Canada—Seigniors.
10. The North-West explored.

1. In 1682 **De la Barre** became Governor, just at a time when there was beginning to be fresh trouble about the fur trade, and the Indians. You were told that the Dutch were the first to settle New York, which they called Manhattan. In 1664 the English got possession of it, and called it **New York**. At the same time, they obtained New Jersey also, and, by their energy, had become great rivals of the French in buying furs from the Indians, not only from the Iroquois, but from the Canadian tribes also. This state of things brought on another Indian war, in which the French were so badly beaten that the king was obliged to send De Denonville, in 1685, to take the place of De la Barre.

2. The war grew so fierce that the French sent an expedition, two years later, all the way to **Hudson Bay**, and seized the small English trading-post there.

3. That one may know how fast the English colonies grew, attention has to be paid to this quarrel between the English and French Governors. When the French marched into what is now New York State, in order to punish the Iroquois, the English Governor, Colonel Dongan, protested against the invasion, because, said he, "It is British ground, and the Iroquois are the allies of the English." Denonville replied, that the French claimed it long before the English settlements were commenced, and that the sovereignty of the Indians inhabiting it, belonged to the king of France. But he did an act which turned the Iroquois forever against France. Having invited their chiefs to a council, he made prisoners of them, and sent them to France. The Indians were so enraged that, although they could not resist the French in battle, they spread through their settlements, burning their houses and barns, and killing the people, so that there was no safety outside of Quebec, Montreal, and Three Rivers. Denonville was obliged to write to the king, and have the chiefs sent back to Canada.

4. Events were occurring at this time in England, which kept that country and France at enmity with each other. To prevent any more misfortunes to Canada, Frontenac was appointed Governor for the second time, in **1689**. He carried on the war in such a manner that the French again had the advantage. His troops and Indians, in the depth of winter, penetrated to the English settlements in Maine, burnt the villages, and killed the people, as the Iroquois had done in Canada.

5. This aroused the English colonies. They met in council at New York, in 1690, and, at their own expense, fitted out **two expeditions** to attack Canada—one, to go by land against Montreal, the other, by sea against Quebec, after taking Acadia. The first reached La Prairie, and was defeated by Frontenac. The second, under Sir William Phipps, took Port Royal in Acadia, but found Quebec too strong, and had to retreat much damaged. These successes so encouraged the French, that, although their crops failed and there was little food, they carried on the war of pillage, as in the former winter. This bitter struggle, known as

"King William's war," was brought to a close by the **Treaty of Ryswick**, 1697. In the following year, Frontenac died, in the 78th year of his age, and the 21st of his rule, respected by both friends and foes. He was buried at Quebec.

6. The next Governor was **De Calliéres**, in 1699. He made a strong treaty with the Iroquois and other tribes, at Montreal, where the chiefs all met. These could not write their names, but instead, each one made a rude sketch of the particular animal which the tribe adopted for its sign. One chief drew a spider, another a bear, or a beaver, as the case might be. In 1701, the Canadians formed a settlement at **Detroit**.

7. In 1703, when the **Marquis de Vaudreuil** became Governor, war again broke out between the English and French, both in Europe and America. Queen Anne at this time ruled England, and Louis XIV., France. You will say, that there was little else but war, and you will say truly. First, the French and Indians, as you have read in the former chapters, and now the English, French, and Indians. It is not pleasant to have to tell of these sad times, and it is hard to believe that people, whose children now live as brethren under the same government, were once shedding each other's blood. We should be glad that we live in peace with our neighbors, and that other means of settling troubles have been found, besides going to war. But still it is necessary to tell that these things did happen, and what came of them.

8. This contest was called "Queen Anne's war," and lasted ten years. At this time, Canada could only muster 4,500 fighting men, while the Atlantic colonies had 60,000. The object of the English colonists was to take Canada, so as not to have an enemy so close to them, as the French on the St. Lawrence and in Acadia. Their plan was similar to that in the former war, a land army to attack Montreal, and a fleet to sail against Quebec. In America, the English lost Newfoundland and failed in all their attacks, except in Acadia; but in Europe, the French were continually defeated, so that when a **treaty** was made at **Utrecht** in 1713, the King of France gave up to England, Acadia, Newfoundland, the Hudson Bay Territory, and the sovereignty over the Iroquois.

9. During the period of peace that now commenced, Canada improved very fast. For its better government it had been divided into three districts, Quebec, Montreal, and Three Rivers. These were now divided into eighty-two parishes. Many of the officers who had come out from France, at different times, were induced to settle in Canada. They received the title of **Seigniors**, and were granted large tracts of land. Many of the parishes in the Province of Quebec still retain the names of the old Seigniors. A census was taken which returned the whole population as twenty-five thousand, seven thousand of these belonging to Quebec, and three thousand to Montreal. Greater care was bestowed upon the cultivation of the land, so that the people raised more than enough to support themselves, and were able to send the surplus to Europe. The **exports** to France included furs, lumber, staves, tar, tobacco, flour, peas, and pork ; while the imports were wines, brandies, linen and woollen goods. In 1723, nineteen vessels sailed from Quebec, six new merchant ships were built and two men-of-war. The education of the people did not receive that attention it does at the present time. There was no system of schools, and only the larger towns enjoyed this advantage.

10. Vaudreuil died in 1725, after governing the province for twenty-one years. He was succeeded the following year by the **Baron de Beauharnois**. In 1731, a party of Montreal merchants explored the regions now called Manitoba and Keewatin. They built several trading-forts, one of which, near Winnipeg, was called **Fort Maurepas**. The same party explored the Missouri in 1738, and reached the Rocky Mountains in 1743.

CHAPTER V.

COLONIAL WARS—CONQUEST OF CANADA.

1. Boundary lines.
2. English plans.
3. Treaty of Aix-la-Chapelle—Halifax founded.
4. The last French Governor.
5. Braddock's Defeat—Acadians.
6. Montcalm and Wolfe—Louisbourg and Quebec.
7. Quebec surrendered.
8. Surrender of Canada.
9. Treaty of Paris.
10. Terms of Surrender.
11. Pontiac.

1. Trouble was again brewing in Europe, and its influence spread to America, where the colonies of France and England renewed the strife of the former two contests. The direct cause of the war on this continent was the jealousy of the two nations about their **boundaries.** The English now owned Acadia, which they called **Nova Scotia**, while the French still possessed the country north of the Bay of Fundy, and the dispute was, who should have the isthmus connecting the two. In the **valley of the Ohio River** there was a similar difficulty, the French claiming all the country between the Mississippi and the Alleghany Mountains, over which the English were extending their settlements. Hence this war came to be called that of the "Boundary Lines."

2. It lasted fourteen years, and only differed from the others, in the larger forces engaged, the different men who took part in the strife, and that the attacks on the French were made in three quarters instead of two. A fleet was to proceed against Cape Breton and Quebec, one land force against Montreal, and another against the French forts in Ohio, and along the lakes. There was also fighting between the two parties in Nova Scotia. The French fought bravely, as they always did, and won many battles; but the English colonists out-numbered the French, and were assisted by generals and soldiers and ships from England. France had all she could do in Europe, and the result was, that piece by piece the English won all the French territory in America. Let us mention the leading facts briefly.

3. In the first year of the war, 1745, England took Cape Breton, but gave it up again three years afterwards by the

Treaty of Aix-la-Chapelle. In 1747 **De Galissoniere** became Governor. He built a fort at **Rouillé** or **Toronto**, and another where Ogdensburgh stands, as a connecting link between Cataraqui, or Frontenac, and Montreal. He also organized a Militia, and found the number to be 10,000. In 1748, he induced a large number of the French inhabitants of Nova Scotia to leave British rule, and live under the French in **Isle St. Jean**, now **Prince Edward Island.** To supply the place of the Acadians, and also to found the settlement of **Halifax**, three thousand eight hundred colonists came out from Britain in 1749. The city of Halifax took its name from the Earl of Halifax, who acted as patron to the colony at this period in its history.

4. In this year **De la Jonquiere** arrived at Quebec as Governor. He received his appointment some three years before, but on his way to Canada was taken prisoner, and only now released. He would have made a good ruler if he had not been so greedy of gain. The Intendant **Bigot** was worse than the Governor. Between the two, Canada fared very badly; the people were refused payment for their produce, and the troops left unsupplied. In 1752 the **Marquis du Quesne** was made Governor. In this year two ships laden with wheat were sent to France, being the first exportation of this grain from the province. Du Quesne strove to carry out many useful reforms, but was constantly opposed by Bigot. He asked to be recalled, and, in 1755, was succeeded by the Marquis de Vaudreuil, who was the last French Governor of Canada. During the winter the French were in a bad condition from want of food.

5. In this year, 1755, the English, under General Braddock, suffered a severe defeat in the Ohio Valley. But they gained some successes at Lake Champlain, and in Nova Scotia. In the latter province, however, the Acadians or French inhabitants, had refused, since their conquest, to take the English oath of allegiance, and still showed their gladness over French victories. The Governor and his Council therefore determined to put them on ships, and disperse them among the English colonies along the Atlantic coast. This was done, but, in some instances, in a very harsh way, for besides being taken from their homes, husbands and wives, parents and children were sent away in

different ships; and thus separated, many never found one another again.

6. **General Montcalm** was sent out, in 1756, to take command of the French troops in Canada, and by his ability prolonged the struggle a few years more. Two years after, England sent out Generals **Wolfe** and **Amherst**, and several other officers, with large forces and a fleet. In 1758 the British took the fortress of **Louisbourg** in Cape Breton, for the last time. In the Ohio Valley they also gained possession of the country, so that in the succeeding year they were able to direct all their armies and fleet against Montreal and Quebec. While General Amherst attempted to conquer the French forts at Lake Champlain, and General Johnson the fort at Niagara, General Wolfe proceeded to the conquest of **Quebec**. With a large fleet bearing his army, he arrived at the Island of Orleans in June, 1759. A long and desperate siege commenced, and lasted until the 13th of September. During the preceding night, the English had succeeded in scaling the rugged heights leading to the **Plains of Abraham**. Here a short and bloody battle ensued on the 13th, which decided the fate of Canada. Wolfe and Montcalm were both mortally wounded. The former died on the battle-field, the latter a few hours later within Quebec.

7. On the 17th the keys of the city were surrendered, and the English army took possession of what was now almost a heap of ruins. General Murray at once set about putting the city in a state of defence, and preparing for the winter. The French troops outside of Quebec, under General de Lévis, retreated to Montreal, where De Vaudreuil had taken up his headquarters. While these events were transpiring on the St. Lawrence, the French forts on the Niagara and in the Ohio Valley had fallen into the hands of the English.

8. Early in the spring, **De Lévis** attempted to retake Quebec. A **second battle** was fought on the Plains of Abraham, in which three thousand English were beaten by seven thousand French. General Murray shut himself within the city, while De Lévis was obliged to retreat again to Montreal, for the British fleet was coming up the river. In July, Murray left Quebec with all the force he could spare, in order to join General Amherst

before Montreal. Seventeen thousand British surrounded this city in September, and De Vaudreuil seeing it was useless to resist longer, **surrendered all Canada** to General Amherst on the 8th of that month, 1760.

9. By the **Treaty of Paris**, in 1763, France assented to the cession of her possessions in North America, with the exception of the islands of **Miquelon** and **St. Pierre** in the Gulf of St. Lawrence, which she yet keeps as stations for her vessels fishing on the Banks of Newfoundland.

10. The terms of surrender were, that the French Canadians should retain possession of their homes, goods, and chattels, enjoy the free exercise of their religion, and have all the civil and commercial rights of British subjects. All who had engaged in the war were pardoned, and the Indians friendly to the French left undisturbed in the possession of their lands.

11. Until this Treaty was made known, the Indian allies of the French in the west were not willing to believe that their friends had lost all power. Early in 1763, Pontiac, a noted chief, at the head of several tribes, nearly carried out a scheme to recapture the frontier forts from the English. Forts Detroit, Niagara, and Pittsburg were the only ones able to resist the savage attacks. Seven others were taken, and the inhabitants either killed or made prisoners. In 1764 the conspiracy was quelled, and Pontiac fled.

CHAPTER VI.

CANADA A CROWN COLONY OF GREAT BRITAIN—THE QUEBEC ACT—
U. E. LOYALISTS.

1. Military rule.
2. English law introduced.
3, 4. Quebec Act.
5. Causes of American Revolution.
6. " United States."
7. Character of the war.
8. Canada invaded.
9. Treaty of Versailles.
10. United Empire Loyalists.
11. Upper Canada and New Brunswick.

1. As soon as the articles of surrender were signed at Montreal, in 1760, General Amherst, as the commander of the English army, became Governor-General of Canada. He divided the country into the three districts of Quebec, Three Rivers, and Montreal. General Murray was appointed to Quebec, and given the duties of

Lieutenant-Governor over Canada ; Colonel Burton was appointed to Three Rivers, and General Gage to Montreal. Each of these was assisted by a council composed of military officers, which decided all cases brought before it, subject to the approval of the Lieutenant-Governor. This form of Government, which is called **military rule**, lasted from 1760 to 1774. It is not always the most pleasant to a people, but, at this time, it was the best that could be given to Canada. The French Canadians were not unhappy under it, for they had never had a voice as to how they should be governed, and had always been obliged to do as their own governors or intendants bade them. Besides, the English brought money with them and paid for what they got, whereas, during the years of the late wars, the Intendant Bigot paid them only in paper money, which the French Court afterwards refused to honor. This difference of treatment by France and England had a great effect in leading the French Canadians to prefer English rule.

2. In 1763, the form of law and the courts which are so much prized in England were introduced into Canada ; but the change was not agreeable, for the French could not understand either the language or the justice of English law. General Murray strove to make its operation as mild as possible, yet there were many complaints.

3. In 1766, the Hon. Guy Carleton succeeded General Murray, and proved also a great friend to the French Canadians, who were constantly asking to have their old laws restored to them. Governor Carleton recommended the English Government to make the "Custom of Paris" the law of Canada, and, after several years of delay, the British Parliament in 1774 passed an Act for this purpose, called the **Quebec Act.** By it the boundaries of the province were made to include Labrador to the east, the settlements in the Ohio valley to the south-west, and all the country to the north as far as Hudson Bay Territory. It permitted the French Canadians to hold office in the colony. In addition to the **Custom of Paris,** the English law regarding criminals was to be enforced. The Governor was to appoint a council of not less than seventeen nor more than twenty-three members, to be composed of both French and English colonists.

These were to have the power to make any necessary laws, subject, however, to the approval of the sovereign of England.

4. While this Act pleased the French, it displeased the **English settlers,** who had begun to pour into Canada. In the Ohio valley the feeling was very stubborn against it, for there was a population of twenty thousand English in that region, and to them the "Quebec Act" was unjust. But along the St. Lawrence the French were by far the most numerous, and it had become a very important matter that they should be contented just at that time.

5. For many years England had been obliged to wage great wars in Europe and Asia, and these wars had been very expensive. Moreover there was the struggle in America, which lasted fourteen years, and cost much money and many lives. Now, when Canada had been conquered, and the colonies on the Atlantic were thus able to live in peace, England thought it was only right that these colonies should assist towards the expenses which had been incurred, and attempted to **impose a tax** on certain goods brought into America. This act of the Home Government at once divided the people of the old colonies into **two parties,** one of which, called **United Empire Loyalists,** was loyal and willing to submit to the tax; but the other refused to pay it, because, said they, "It is contrary to our freedom that we should pay taxes to the English Government, when we do not send members to the English Parliament. We should have something to say about the voting of our own money." For ten years a quiet resistance was maintained, during which time the English Parliament modified its demands, until a light duty on tea was the only tax levied. But these concessions had no effect. The one party refused to pay even this, and when the Home Government attempted to compel the payment, war broke out in 1775, the year following the passage of the "Quebec Act."

6. The war had only been in progress a year, when the thirteen colonies determined to throw off their **allegiance** to Great Britain altogether, and, at a Congress held at Philadelphia, declared their **independence,** July 4th, 1776, under the name of the **United States.** This Congress invited Canada and the other British provinces to join the "States," but the Provinces refused to do so, and remained steadfast to the British Crown.

7. The war of the "American Revolution" once commenced, was carried on with more bitterness than any that had been fought before in America. It was very sad, because it was between people of the **same blood** and **language**; even families were divided, fathers and sons fighting against one another. What made it so bitter was, that each side claimed to be doing right—the Rebels in not paying the tax, and resisting what they called tyranny—while the Loyalists were ready, not only cheerfully to submit to the law, but also to die in the defence of the Mother Country.

8. The contest began with the skirmish at Lexington, in 1775. In the same year the Americans **invaded Canada**, and got possession of Montreal. On the last day of the year they attempted an assault upon Quebec; but were defeated with the loss of their leader, General Montgomery. During 1776 they were driven out of Canada, and tried no more to take it while the war lasted. In 1778, General Haldimand became Governor of Canada. For six years the fierce strife went on in the thirteen States, until it was ended by the surrender of the British army under Lord Cornwallis, at **Yorktown**, in 1782.

9. Great Britain acknowledged the independence of the thirteen United States by the **Treaty of Versailles**, in 1783, and the boundaries of British America were reduced to their present limits.

10. The party in the States which had remained loyal to England during the late war were now left in a very unpleasant position. England asked the Congress to show them leniency, and Congress did recommend the governments of the several States to treat the Loyalists with kindness; but Congress had not much influence then, and, wherever these people lived, their neighbors looked upon them with great disfavor, and treated them often with great harshness. Many of the Loyalists were very wealthy and had a great deal of property, which was coveted by the victorious party. Victory did not make the latter generous, but they allowed all the bitter feelings of the war to control them, and passed laws **confiscating**, or taking away the property of the Loyalists, and declaring them enemies of the new Government. This act hastened the departure of these brave people from the

territory of the United States. But the greater number gave up their lands and houses of their own accord, preferring to live under the old flag. Many went to England, but more emigrated to the Provinces—about twenty thousand to Nova Scotia and New Brunswick, and ten thousand to what is now the Province of Ontario.

11. From the time that Canada became an English province, up to the year 1784, the **country west** of the River Ottawa had not grown much in population. But in that year Governor Haldimand sent surveyors to lay out in lots the country along the St. Lawrence and Bay of Quinté, and around Niagara and Amherstburg. It grieved the English Government to see the manner in which the Loyalists were treated, and a list of them under the designation of United Empire Loyalists, was ordered to be made. Nearly £4,000,000 sterling was voted to be divided among them, besides large grants of land in the new country. Five thousand acres was the allowance to field-officers, three thousand to captains, two thousand to subalterns, and two hundred to private soldiers, and others; while two hundred acres were to be given to each son on coming of age, and a like number to each daughter whenever she married. They were also given tools for building, implements for tilling the land, seed to sow, and the food and clothing necessary for three years. All this was very generous, but it did not make up for all the Loyalists had been forced to leave behind in their old homes. But they were true men and women, who chose rather to lose all than give up their allegiance to, and love for, the Mother Country. These were the people who laid the foundation of the Provinces of **Upper Canada,** or **Ontario,** and of **New Brunswick.**

CHAPTER VII.
CONSTITUTIONAL ACT, 1791.

1. The Governor-General.
2. Division of Upper Canada.
3. State of Government.
4. Agitation.
5. Two young nations.
6. Land tenures.
7. Seigniors.
8. Freeholder.
9. Two provinces.
10-13. Terms of the Act.

1. In 1785 General Haldimand returned to England, and Henry Hamilton and Colonel Hope administered the government in succession until the next year, when General Carleton, who had been made Lord Dorchester, arrived at Quebec as Governor-General. Since the late war it had become the custom to appoint a **Governor-General**, who represented the English sovereign, and who resided at Quebec and ruled Lower Canada, while Lieutenant-Governors were appointed to the other provinces. It was thought, in this way, to preserve a kind of union among the several provinces.

2. In 1787, the Duke of Clarence, afterwards William IV., visited Canada, and in the following year Lord Dorchester divided the western province into four districts, named Lunenburg, Mecklenburg, Nassau and Hesse, the one farthest to the east being Lunenburg.

3. You have been told how the English governed Canada at first by "Military Rule," from 1760 to 1774, during which the military rulers and their councils of officers tried to do the best they could, in their ignorance of French law and customs. You have seen the efforts made by the English Parliament to make the French contented, and that for this purpose, the "Quebec Act" of 1774 was passed, making **French law** the law of Canada, although the English settlers did not like it. But the French were many times more numerous than the English then, and the "greatest content of the greatest number" must be the excuse of the Home Government. The English settlers had always complained against the "Quebec Act," and their complaints became more frequent after so many U. E. Loyalists came into the country and settled west of the Ottawa.

4. The English Canadians sent **petitions** to the king, asking him to have the Act repealed, while the French Canadians sent petitions to have it retained. The king and his ministers were very much perplexed, but they did nothing hastily. Lord Dorchester was told to find out all he could about the true state of the matter, and what would be best to be done. He divided his council into committees and gave each of these a distinct work to do. One committee had to gather all the information possible about the agriculture and commerce of Canada; another, about the militia; another, about education, and another, about the courts, and how justice was dealt to the inhabitants. This was in 1786. The work was done carefully, and the reports sent to England, for the guidance of the Parliament; in addition, some English, and some French Canadians went to England and told the story of their grievances. By means of this knowledge, the British Government expected to be in a position to settle the complaints of the colonists. Perhaps you may think this a great deal of trouble for a government in England to take about places so far off as Canada. But it is the right way. Law should never be made or changed, without knowing everything possible concerning what the law is intended to do, what evils it will remove, and what benefits it will confer. If laws had been always passed **thus carefully**, the United States might to-day be under British Government.

5. If the Canadians had been either all French or all English, it would have been easier for the king and his ministers to determine what to do. But there were **two young nations** in Canada, a little France that had been growing for two hundred years, and a little England just springing up. Why were the French so eager to keep their old laws? They liked British rule better than that of old France, for they were now freer and more prosperous, and there were some English laws which they preferred; for instance, that against criminals. But the English law regarding land and property was so different from the French law, that the French Canadians were afraid to have it established, lest they should lose their farms, or be disturbed in any way.

6. That you may understand something more on this subject, which is of great importance in Canadian history, let us point out the difference between these two kinds of law. At first all the

land settled by the French was held by **Feudal tenure**, that is, the king always kept the right to it. The holders had to do certain duties as the king desired, and he could at any time bestow the lands on others. With such a law there was little encouragement for people to leave old France and come to the New World. When Richelieu formed the Company of "One Hundred Associates," the law was changed so that colonists held their lands by **Seigniorial tenure**, which means that the land of Canada was divided into portions, and given to gentlemen in favor with the king and Richelieu, or to the religious orders that sent out missionaries. These divisions were not all equal, but varied a great deal, some being as large as a township, and others less or more. For instance, La Salle received the Seigniory of Cataraqui, or Frontenac, Joliette was given the island of Anticosti, and the island of Montreal was bestowed on M. de Lauson in 1635, and passed to the religious order of St. Sulpice in 1664. The Seigniors afterwards divided their portions in lots among those wishing to settle, the holders paying the Seignior certain sums every year.

7. It was after this "tenure" became the law, that Canada grew and increased in population, and all the French owned their land under it. The French Canadians were not used to governing themselves; they depended upon the Seigniors, and looked up to them. No person could take their land from them, for it belonged to the "lord," and they might live upon it as long as they chose. But this was not a good law for the improvement of the country. There were so many ways in which the tenant had to pay the Seignior that the farmer became careless. The more valuable he made his farm by working it well, or erecting good buildings upon it, the more he had to pay, so that he had no motive for making his condition better, or for improving his land.

8. Under the English law, if a man wished to possess land, he bought it and paid for it at once, and received a deed either from the Government, or from the former owner. This deed made him a **freeholder**, that is, he held his land free from all payments, except the usual taxes to the Government. He had no tribute to pay to a Seignior. But if he got into debt, he was liable to have his land taken and sold to pay his debts. The French Canadians were afraid of such a law, for it would make them depend more

upon themselves; and when the English began to come into Canada, with their new ways of farming and their eagerness to possess large farms, the former inhabitants became alarmed, lest they should be crowded out of the country. They were generally attached to the Seigniors, and preferred their old laws, to which they were used, and one cannot blame them. But this very thing had an important effect upon the action of the British Parliament, in trying to arrange the troubles of Canada. If it had not been for these long-established customs in the Lower Province, there would only have been **one Canada**, instead of two separated by the River Ottawa.

9. As it was, however, in 1791, an Act was passed in England called the **Constitutional Act**, which divided Canada into two provinces, the Lower and Upper, separated, as we have just said, by the Ottawa.

10. Each province was to have a Governor of its own, **and a Parliament** consisting of two Houses, namely, an Assembly elected by the people as now, and a Legislative Council whose members were to be selected by the Governor, from the older and more wealthy men of the Province. Moreover, the Governor was to select an Executive Council composed of a few men, to advise him especially. All laws and ordinances made under the Quebec Act were to remain in force, until altered by the new parliaments. The tenure of land in Lower Canada was to be fixed by its local Legislature, while in Upper Canada, where the colonists were mostly of British origin, all lands were to be held by "freehold tenure." This Act of 1791 also sought to provide for the support of a Protestant clergy in both Canadas, by setting apart a large extent of wild lands for that purpose. These lands were called **Clergy Reserves**, and were afterwards a source of much contention, as you shall read further on.

11. With regard to taxes, the British Government retained in its own hands the right to impose duties for the regulation of trade and commerce; but the Canadian parliaments had the power to collect these, and also to tax themselves for the building of public works, such as roads and bridges, and for education.

12. In Lower Canada the House of Assembly was to have fifty members, and the Legislative Council fifteen. In Upper Canada

the former was to have sixteen members, and the latter seven. A census of the whole country was taken at this time, which showed the population to be 150,000, of which 20,000 belonged to Upper Canada.

13. This Act took effect in the two provinces on the 26th of December, 1791. Lord Dorchester had at this time returned to England, and General Clarke acted as Lieutenant-Governor.

CHAPTER VIII.

LOWER CANADA UNDER A PARLIAMENT.

1. Elective Parliament.
2. The functions of Parliament.
3. Parliamentary terms.
4. First Parliament.
5. General condition of things.
6. Jesuit estates.
7. Slavery.
8. Alien Bill.
9. Steamboats.
10. Signs of war.

1. Let us review the changes in the government of Canada subsequent to 1760. *First,* England held Canada by military occupation from 1760, until the Treaty of Paris confirmed her right to the latter. *Secondly,* from 1763 to 1791, Canada's relation to England was that of a Crown colony, that is, a colony which is not governed by an elective parliament of its own, but by governors acting under instructions from the Home Government. The "Quebec Act" only modified the terms of this relation, but did not remove it.

The **third great change** was made by the Act of 1791. By it *elective* parliaments were introduced, for the first time, into this part of British America. But a similar form of government had already been given to Nova Scotia in 1758; and to New Brunswick in 1784, when it became a separate province.

2. It is important for us, then, to know something about the meaning of the word "parliament," and about what is done in parliament. The name comes from a French word meaning *to talk*, and you have before been told how the Canadian Parliament was to be composed. The members of the Assembly were elected to serve four years. The two Houses do not sit together, but in separate chambers, to talk over the affairs of the country, and to make laws. It has never been necessary for the Parliament to

continue its meeting throughout the whole of the four years, but only for a few weeks or months of each year, and this period of time is called a **session**. When it meets, each House is presided over by a **Speaker**, who is one of its members, and directs its actions while in session. The records of the debates and doings of each day are called the **minutes**, and these must be entered in books kept for the purpose, and called the journals of the House. When any member wishes to propose a law, which he thinks ought to be made, he must first ask leave to propose it, and does so by writing a short statement of what he wants. This written request is called a **motion**, and must be signed by the proposer and another member, who thus become the **mover** and **seconder** of it. As soon as the House grants the motion, the mover brings in a more lengthy statement of the proposed law, telling everything about it, and drawn up after a regular form. This longer statement is called a **bill**. In order to become law a bill must be passed, or agreed to, by both Houses, and receive the assent of the Governor. It is then called an **Act of Parliament**, becomes **law**, and must be obeyed. If a bill does not become law, it is said to be defeated. This may be done in three ways. It may not be agreed to in the House where it was first moved, or it may pass there and not be agreed to in the other, or the Governor may not give his assent after it has passed both Houses.

3. There are three ways of closing the business of a session, either by adjourning, proroguing, or dissolving Parliament. When it is **adjourned**, the members are dismissed, to meet again at a certain time, when they resume any unfinished business, as if there had been no adjournment. To **prorogue** Parliament is to stop all its work, and any business not completed must be taken up afterwards, as if nothing had been done about it. But when Parliament is **dissolved**, not only is its business ended, there must also be a **new election**, before it can come together again.

4. The first Parliament of Lower Canada met at Quebec on the 17th of December, 1792. Of the fifty members elected to the Assembly only fifteen were of British origin, so that it became necessary to decide whether French or English was to be spoken in the House. It was agreed that each member should have the privilege of speaking in either language, but that all motions, and the minutes of Parliament, should be written in both languages.

5. The new order of things gave an impulse to the country, which now began to make steady progress. New roads were opened up, and the navigation of the St. Lawrence was improved. At this time it took four months for a mail to go from Canada to England and return, in the sailing vessels which then crossed the ocean. In 1792, there was a monthly mail between Halifax and Quebec, and seven years afterwards, a weekly mail passed between Montreal and the United States. Lord Dorchester returned to Canada in 1793, and remained until 1796, when General Prescott became Governor-General. Sir Robert Milnes succeeded him in 1799.

6. When the English took Canada they **confiscated** the estates or seigniories of the religious order called Jesuits. In 1800, the revenues of these estates were devoted to education, which about that time received more attention.

7. The practice of keeping **slaves** had been brought into the province by people who came from the United States, where it had been in vogue for a long time. The feelings of Canadians were not in favor of the practice, and it was passing away as fast as circumstances would permit. There were at this time three hundred slaves in Lower Canada. No Act of Parliament was passed against slavery in that province, but in 1803 Chief Justice Osgoode declared in court that it was not consistent with the laws of the country. People saw that the courts would not uphold them in keeping slaves, and as a consequence the blacks received their freedom.

8. The first English cathedral was built at Quebec in 1804. Sir James Craig assumed the duties of Governor-General in 1807. In the meantime the people took a great interest in the actions of the Government, and there was often a good deal of bitterness between the two races, both in and out of Parliament. Several newspapers had also been published in both French and English, and these kept up the strife even when the Parliament was not in session. Some people in the United States thought this a favorable time to spread disloyalty among Canadians, and many strangers were found throughout the country trying to teach rebellion. But the Parliament passed the **Alien Bill**, which was an Act to punish aliens, or people of other countries, found guilty

of such sedition. As there was much bad feeling springing up in the United States against England, a Militia Act was also passed for the safety of Canada, while Sir James Craig made a tour through the Province and everywhere received the assurance of the loyal feelings of the people.

9. The trade of the world was about to get a new impulse from the **use of steam** in navigation, and young Canada was not behind the other nations in applying it to boats upon her rivers. The first steamboat, of which there is any record, was one buit by Symington, a Scotchman, in 1802, and which was used on the Forth and Clyde Canal; the second and third were launched upon the Hudson River by Fulton, in 1805, and 1809. In the latter year, the **Hon. John Molson**, a wealthy merchant of Montreal, built a steamboat on the St. Lawrence. On the 3rd of November, it started down the river, and made the voyage to Quebec in thirty-six hours. A newspaper of that city gave a description of the little boat which excited great wonder in those days. The paper said : "The steamboat 'Accommodation' has arrived with ten passengers. She is incessantly crowded with visitors. This steamboat receives her impulse from an open-spoked perpendicular wheel on each side, without any circular band or rim ; to the end of each double spoke is fixed a square board which enters the water, and, by the rotary motion of the wheels, acts like a paddle. No wind nor tide can stop her. The price of a passage is nine dollars up, and eight down." Such was the first Canadian steamboat.

10. Sir George Prevost became Governor-General in 1811. During this and the preceding year, the trouble between the United States and England grew worse and worse, and **signs of war** began to appear ; but, before speaking of this, let us see what Upper Canada had been doing since she became a separate province in 1791.

CHAPTER IX.

UPPER CANADA A SEPARATE PROVINCE.

1, 2. Social condition.
3. First Parliament.
4. Slavery.
5. London—York.
6. Custom duties—Trade.
7. Sir Isaac Brock.

1. When Upper Canada was first made a **separate province** in 1791, it had only a small and thinly scattered population of some twenty thousand people. These were to be found along the St. Lawrence, the Bay of Quinté, the Niagara frontier, and the Detroit River. Small villages were to be found at Kingston, Newark or Niagara, and Amherstburg. All the rest of the country was a **wilderness**, covered with forests of fine, large timber. The early settler went into the forest with very few goods, except the clothes on his back, a flint-lock musket, and an axe. Some had not even these, and all were more or less obliged to accept the help, which the Government offered to them when "drawing" their land. This help consisted of food and clothes for three years, or until the settlers were able to provide these for themselves. They were also given seeds to sow on their "clearings," and such tools as they might require. Each family received an axe, a hoe and a spade ; a plough and one cow were given to every two families ; large saws to every fourth family, and even boats were furnished for their use and placed at suitable points on the rivers. As there were no mills, even this want was supplied in part by the distribution of "portable corn-mills" made of steel plates, and turned by hand like a coffee-mill. Where the people had not these mills, they used to place the grain in the hollow of a hardwood stump or log, and pound it fine by means of a heavy stone swung above, so as to be easily lifted and lowered.

2. A log house was first built. This was done by the skilful use of the axe, and the help of the nearest neighbors. A small clearing was then made and the fallen timber burnt to leave the land free for tillage. Here the pioneer planted his first seed, and while awaiting the harvest, he extended his clearing by chopping and burning ; then fencing it in, prepared it for larger crops. Burning

the fallen trees was sometimes very dangerous, for if the woods caught fire the flames spread very swiftly and very far, causing the poor settlers to flee for their lives. Many brave men and women, thrust out from homes of comfort and plenty after the war of the Revolution, made for themselves new homes in the Canadian forest. By industry their little possessions increased, their stock multiplied, and the lonely families after a time had all things needful for living. These were perhaps coarse in quality, but abundant in quantity, and the best for health and strength. In course of time they produced their own clothing. The skilful fingers of the housewife and her daughters worked the flax and wool through all the stages of preparation, and, weaving them in their own houses, made good strong clothes which would endure wear and tear. The table also of the Canadian settler had its good things, for deer roamed through the forest, and the rivers teemed with fish, several kinds of which we do not now see at all, while wild ducks, geese and pigeons often fell victims to the old musket, which may already have done duty in by-gone wars.

3. The Province had, since its settlement in 1784, been under the government of the Legislative Council of Lower Canada, which was founded by the Quebec Act. But in 1791, Upper Canada stood by itself, as an infant colony, with the privilege of making its own laws. Colonel John Graves Simcoe became the first Lieutenant-Governor in the following year. He selected the village of **Niagara** or **Newark** as his headquarters for the time, until he should be able to select a place more suitable for a permanent capital. There he opened his first Parliament, on the 17th of September, 1792, in what was little better than a log house. The House of Assembly consisted of sixteen members, the Legislative Council of seven, while the Executive Council was composed of five members, appointed to advise and aid the Governor. The plain, honest men who formed this primitive parliament went to work in making laws to govern the country, as earnestly as they did in chopping its forests and clearing the land. They wasted no time in useless debate, and two months before the Parliament of Lower Canada had met, they had finished their work of law-making, and returned home. They made the **civil law of England** the law of the Province ; introduced trial by

UPPER CANADA A SEPARATE PROVINCE. 53

jury; provided for the recovery of small debts, and fixed the toll for millers at one-twelfth for grinding and bolting. They changed the name of the districts into which Lord Dorchester had divided the Province, and called them the Eastern or Johnstown District, the Midland or Kingston, the Home or Niagara, and the Western or Detroit; and these were again divided into twelve counties. An Act was also passed to erect a jail and court-house in each of these districts.

4. In the next year, the second session began in May, and was marked by the passing of other useful Acts. One offered a reward for the killing of wolves and bears, which shows that the number of these animals was large enough to prove a source of trouble to the early settlers. The most important Act was that doing away with **slavery**, forbidding the bringing of any more slaves into the province, and making all slave-children free at the age of twenty-five. The elections for the House of Assembly were held every four years, and the first Parliament held its last session in 1795. The first Upper Canadian newspaper, the *Gazette*, was started during this period.

5. In the meantime, Colonel Simcoe was trying to select a better place than Newark for the seat of Government, for Newark was too near the frontier of another country. He was in favor of going farther west, and for this purpose chose the site of the present city of **London**, which he named, calling the river on which it was situated the Thames. But the Governor-General, Lord Dorchester, wished to make Kingston the capital. Thus the two governors could not agree, and at last Colonel Simcoe fixed upon the site of the old French fort, Rouillé, now Toronto. Here he pitched his tent until block-houses could be built for himself and his soldiers, whom he employed in making roads. In 1795 there were only twelve houses, besides the barracks, in **York**, as it was then called.

6. In 1796, Governor Simcoe was recalled, and the Hon. Peter Russell, President of the Executive Council, acted in his place. The government offices were now moved to York, and the Parliament was opened there in the same year. When the two provinces were separated, they agreed to divide between them the **revenue** collected at the ports of Quebec and Montreal, Upper Canada to

receive **one-eighth**, which was thought to equal her share of the import trade, and therefore of the duties. This eighth amounted, in 1796, to five thousand dollars. The trade of a country is a good index to the way in which the country is making progress. In thirteen years this eighth increased to twenty-eight thousand dollars, and Upper Canada's share was changed to one-fifth, showing how prosperous both provinces were becoming. But besides the trade by way of Lower Canada, a direct commerce had rapidly grown up between the Western Province and the State of New York, so that it became necessary to open ten **ports of entry**, which extended from Cornwall on the St. Lawrence, to Sandwich on the Detroit River. In 1799, General Hunter arrived in the province, and replaced Mr. Russell at the head of the Government. Meanwhile the province was rapidly growing in population as well as wealth, and, for so young a country, showed a vigorous spirit of enterprise. The Hon. Francis Gore became Lieutenant-Governor in 1806, and in the following year the Parliament granted the liberal sum of £800 for the purpose of paying the salaries of masters of **Grammar schools**, one of which was founded in each of the eight districts into which Upper Canada had by this time become divided; and in 1810, a first grant of £2,000 was made for the building of roads and bridges.

7. In 1811, a census was taken, which gave the population as seventy-seven thousand. In the same year, Mr. Gore returned to England, and General **Sir Isaac Brock** took charge of the Government at the same time that Sir George Prevost took up his residence at Quebec as Governor-General.

CHAPTER X.

WAR OF 1812, '13, AND '14.

1. War declared.
2, 3. Feeling in Canada.
4. Precautions.
5. Mackinaw—Detroit.
6. Queenston Heights.
7. Lacolle River.
8. Army-bills.
9. American plans.
10. Overland march.
11. York taken.
12. Fort George taken.
13. Retreat at Sackett's Harbor.
14. Sir James Yeo.
15. Stony Creek.
16. Heroism—Beaver Dams.
17. Lake Erie—Moraviantown.
18. Chrysler's Farm.
19. Chateauguay.
20. Niagara burnt.
21. Reprisals.
22. Winter work.
23. Lacolle Mill.
24. Oswego.
25. Chippewa.
26. Lundy's Lane.
27. Fort Erie.
28. Maine.
29. Plattsburg.
30. Treaty of Ghent.

1. In 1812, war was declared between England and the United States. For three years the cruel strife went on, and much innocent and brave blood was spilled on the soil of Canada, where the people had done nothing to cause the war, their only fault being that they preferred to live as a province of Great Britain, rather than join their lot to the States, which had succeeded in throwing off the control of the Mother Country. All the States were not in favor of the war; but there was a large party, the ruling party then, which hated England, and which had, for several years, been anxious to pick a quarrel with her. This party talked a great deal about liberty, and yet had no sympathy with England in her contest with Napoleon, for the liberty not only of Europe but also of her own island kingdom. Great Britain tried to satisfy the complaints of these discontented Americans, but with no avail; their Congress **declared war** on the 18th of June, 1812, and England was forced on her part to declare war on the 13th of the following October.

2. For several months previous to the 18th of June, Upper Canadians knew that, though they had done nothing to bring war upon themselves, the United States would **invade** the provinces. They felt that the **real object** of the war party was to gain Canada, and make it another State of the Union. They resolved not to submit, but brave'y to fight for their new homes and for

their honor as British subjects. The U. E. Loyalists thought of all the wrongs they had already suffered from the same party during the Revolution, and the memory of those wrongs only made them the more ready to defend themselves and their little ones to the last.

3. In Lower Canada the feeling of the French was just as strong to fight against the enemies of England. Since 1774, they had learned that England meant to keep her promises to them; since 1791, they had tasted the pleasure of governing themselves, and had begun to enjoy a liberty which they felt they would lose if conquered again.

4. In Upper and Lower Canada, therefore, as early as February, measures were taken so as not to be surprised. England, being engaged in a war against Napoleon in Europe, could not spare any troops for Canada, and in both provinces there were only 4,500 regular soldiers. But the **militia** turned out promptly to be drilled, while the parliaments voted all the money they could. In the Upper Province the population was much scattered, yet the militia used to meet six times a month to drill, some of them walking many miles through the woods to perform this duty.

5. Upper Canada was the first to be invaded. General Hull, the Governor of Michigan, crossed the Detroit River on the 12th of July, with 2,500 men, and attacked **Fort Malden**, near Amherstburg, garrisoned by three hundred British regulars under Colonel St. George. But he did not succeed. Colonel Proctor captured his convoy of provisions and cut off his supplies, while Captain Roberts took **Fort Mackinaw**, situated between Lakes Huron and Michigan. These things made Hull uneasy. When the news of the invasion came to York the Legislature was in session, but General Brock dismissed the members and set out at once for Amherstburg with only seven hundred men. After a toilsome journey by land and water, he reached that place on the 13th of September, and there met the great Indian Chief Tecumseh, with six hundred of his warriors. Meanwhile Hull had retreated to **Detroit**, whither Brock followed with his little force of seven hundred men. As Hull saw him advance his heart failed him, and he hoisted the white flag in token of surrender. General Brock allowed the American militia to return to their homes, but the regulars and officers, more than one thousand men, were sent

prisoners to Quebec. The British thus got large quantities of stores and provisions, and the whole State of Michigan passed into their hands. The chief result of this victory was, that it raised the confidence of the Canadians, and secured the fidelity of the Indians, who hated the "Long Knives," as they called the Americans.

6. On the morning of the 13th of October, the Americans, under General VanRensselaer, crossed the Niagara River and attacked **Queenston**. Here a great struggle took place, first one side and then the other gaining the advantage. Early in the battle, **General Brock**, and a Canadian officer, **Colonel Macdonell**, were killed, but this only made the small party of British more determined, and at last the Americans were driven back, many of them over the steep river bank, and the rest, 950 in number, surrendered. In November another attempt to cross the river was defeated.

7. In this month General Dearborn invaded Lower Canada by way of Lake Champlain, but he also was defeated by **Colonel de Salaberry** at **Lacolle** River. Thus the attempts to take Canada in the year 1812 proved failures.

8. In 1813, General Sheaffe succeeded General Brock in the Upper Province. Both parliaments met for short sessions, and passed Acts giving more money for maintaining the defence of the country. But to prevent the coin going out of Canada, they issued paper money called **Army-bills**, like bank-notes of the present day, only that these could not be exchanged for coin until the end of the war.

9. The Americans kept up the contest during the winter. They hoped, by striking Canada in several quarters at the same time, to divide her small forces, and thus gain an easy victory. They threatened our frontier with **three armies**, one in the west under General Harrison; one along the Niagara River, under General Dearborn, and a third near Lower Canada commanded by General Hampton.

10. In the depth of winter the 104th British regiment marched overland from New Brunswick.

11. Colonel Proctor was very active, and with his small band kept General Harrison at bay for several months. At Prescott,

on the St. Lawrence, Major Macdonell, with what force he could collect, marched across the ice, and after a sharp struggle captured **Ogdensburg**, getting as a reward a large quantity of stores and arms, which were much needed, for there had not been muskets enough in Canada to give a gun to each man of the militia. Early in the spring, both sides began to build vessels on the lakes for the purpose of carrying on the war. The Americans were able to take the lead in this enterprise, so that on the 25th of April fourteen vessels left Sackett's Harbor, with two thousand men under General Dearborn, for an attack on **York**, which was guarded by only six hundred British regulars and militia. Against such odds York could not stand long, but before it was surrendered, the Americans had to fight every foot of the way into the only fort that the place had. Two hundred and ninety-three militia were taken prisoners, General Sheaffe having retreated in time towards Kingston, taking the regulars with him. For his remissness in the defence of York, this officer was removed to Lower Canada, General de Rottenburg taking his place in the Upper Province.

12. From York the Americans sailed to the mouth of the Niagara River. Here were two forts opposite to one another, one on each side of the river—Fort Niagara on the American side, and **Fort George** on the British side. General Vincent held the latter with fourteen hundred men. When General Dearborn approached this fort with his fleet, General Vincent had very little ammunition, but as long as it lasted he kept the Americans from landing, driving them off three times. At last he was obliged to spike the cannon of the fort, blow up the magazine, and retreat towards Queenston. The following day, having withdrawn the garrisons from Fort Erie, and other posts along the river, he continued his retreat to **Burlington Heights**. His force was now reduced to sixteen hundred men. In the defence of Fort George he had lost about four hundred in killed, wounded and prisoners; while in the assault the Americans had thirty-nine killed, and one hundred and eleven wounded.

13. While Fort George was being bombarded, Sir George Prevost left Kingston with seven vessels, crossed the lake to **Sackett's Harbor**, and did a good deal of damage to the

Americans, but failed to take the place, much to the disappointment of the officers and men, who were ordered to retreat just when they were on the point of victory. But Sir George Prevost, although a good governor in time of peace, was too undecided to make a good general.

14. At this time there arrived out from England a naval officer named **Sir James Yeo**, who brought with him four hundred and fifty seamen and several officers, for the purpose of manning the British vessels on the lakes. He left Kingston on the third of June with two hundred and eighty regulars and some supplies for General Vincent. These numbers are mentioned in order to show you how small the resources of the Province were, when only so few men could be spared for such an important position as the peninsula between Lakes Erie and Ontario.

15. But before aid reached him, General Vincent had turned his retreat into a great success. A few days after his retreat nearly four thousand Americans had followed him and encamped at Stony Creek, six miles distant. General Vincent sent Colonel Harvey to observe what the enemy were doing. This officer, seeing the carelessness with which they guarded their camp, proposed a night surprise. General Vincent assented, and Harvey with seven hundred men set out at midnight of the 5th of June for the American camp. The attack was a complete surprise, for though some stood their ground and fought bravely, the most of the enemy ran away in all directions. Harvey, not wishing the smallness of his force to be seen, withdrew before daylight, taking with him four cannon and one hundred and twenty prisoners, including both their generals, Winder and Chandler. When day broke the fugitives returned to their camp, destroyed their stores, and retreated hastily to the mouth of Forty-mile Creek, where they were joined by another American force of two thousand advancing to their support. Here a camp was formed, before which Sir James Yeo appeared on the 8th. After a short cannonade the Americans retreated to Fort George, leaving their tents standing, and their wounded and provisions to be taken possession of by Vincent's advanced guard. Twelve bateaux laden with baggage were also captured.

16. You see by the narrative of the war thus far, how determined the Americans were to get Canada, and how the Canadians were

just as determined to resist the invaders. The enemy had everything, cannon, arms, ammunition, warm uniforms, and provisions constantly furnished to them from their own country; on the other side, only the few British regulars were fully armed. The militia left their homes to be taken care of by their wives and younger children, and the fathers and elder sons went out to protect them by fighting on the frontier. Without uniforms, armed with flint-lock muskets, sometimes with little ammunition, they went away to do their duty at the front. Many deeds of heroism were performed, not only in the ranks, as related here, but also by individuals. Indeed the defence of Canada, during these three years, was as heroic as any of the struggles of which you may read in history. The women were not a whit less brave than the men. As an instance may be related the long walk of twenty miles through the woods, made by **Mrs. Secord**, to warn the British out-post at a place called **Beaver Dams**. After the battle of Stony Creek, Dearborn had sent a force of six hundred men to surprise the camp at Beaver Dams, but the latter, through the timely warning of this brave lady, was able to compel the Americans to surrender. General Vincent in his turn besieged the Americans shut up in Fort George.

17. In September the British suffered a severe defeat on **Lake Erie**, where Commodore **Perry** with nine American vessels captured the six British vessels under Captain Barclay. This compelled Proctor and Tecumseh to leave Detroit and retreat into Canada, closely followed by Harrison with four times their force. The latter harassed Proctor's rear, so that he was obliged to make a stand at **Moraviantown**. Wearied and destitute, the six hundred British and five hundred Indians could not make a long resistance against the four thousand Americans. Tecumseh was killed, while Proctor and all who could, escaped through the forest to join General Vincent.

18. Elated by these successes, the invaders thought they would make a great effort against **Montreal**. For this purpose they assembled nine thousand troops at Sackett's Harbor under General Wilkinson, who was to take Kingston and Prescott, and thus leave the way clear for Harrison to follow, while he went on to join another army under Hampton, who was to approach Montreal by

way of Lake Champlain. But Wilkinson, afraid to attack Kingston, passed it by and descended the St. Lawrence, while the Canadians followed along the bank to watch the American army, which was embarked in more than three hundred boats and schooners. So much was Wilkinson harassed by the British cannon from the land, and the few gunboats that kept close to the rear of his fleet, that he was obliged to land two thousand of his troops at Williamsburg, in order to beat off his assailants. But after two hours of severe fighting, they were obliged to seek their boats and cross to their own side of the river. This battle is known as that of **Crysler's Farm**, in which the British had only one thousand engaged, under Colonel Morrison.

19. On Lake Champlain the British were successful in capturing American shipping, and in burning Plattsburg. This was in 1813. Again, in September, Colonel de Salaberry, with four hundred brave French Canadians, defeated Hampton, with three thousand Americans, who were on their way to join Wilkinson. This victory of **Chateauguay** saved Montreal, and ended the campaign in Lower Canada for the year.

20. In Upper Canada, however, General Vincent had been obliged to fortify himself at Burlington Heights, while the Americans scoured the peninsula, carrying off the provisions and cattle of the inhabitants, and burning their buildings. The village of **Niagara** was burned, only one house remaining out of one hundred and fifty. The winter of 1813 was very severe, and the night of the 10th of December, when this act was done, was one of the most bitter of the season. The villagers were given half an hour to leave, and with what they could gather in that short time, were turned out in the cold, to see their homes consumed by the flames.

21. Shortly afterwards, General Drummond, who had been appointed to the control of Upper Canada, arrived at General Vincent's headquarters; and Colonel Murray was sent to attack **Fort Niagara**, which he took, capturing three hundred prisoners. Another officer, General Riall, took **Lewiston** on the American side, and committed it to the flames, in retaliation for the burning of the Canadian village. Three other American villages were also burnt. So angry were the British at the way in which the Americans had treated the people's homes in Canada,

that they in their turn swept over the American country between the lakes, spreading terror wherever they went. The inhabitants of **Buffalo** fled at the first warning, and the British burnt that town also and much of the shipping. This happened on the last day of the year 1813.

22. In 1814, as the Americans still kept up their forces along the border, it became necessary for the Legislature to vote more money, and take further measures for the defence of the country. During the winter, all kinds of necessary stores were conveyed by sleighs from Montreal to Kingston and Toronto; and another battalion of **regulars, with** two hundred and fifty sailors, marched overland through the woods from New Brunswick.

23. In March, General Wilkinson led five thousand men against five hundred British posted at **Lacolle Mill** in Lower Canada. For more than four hours these kept at bay that large force, after which the American general beat a retreat to Plattsburg.

24. In May, General Drummond, with Yeo's fleet, embarked a force of twelve hundred men for an attack on **Oswego.** Its defenders were dispersed, the forts destroyed, and large quantities of stores carried off.

25. On the Niagara frontier the Americans had been massing a large force, and, on the 3rd of July, Generals Ripley and Scott, with an army four thousand strong, crossed the river, and received the surrender of Fort Erie, held by only one hundred and seventy British. They then pushed on towards Chippewa. To resist this invasion General Riall had not two thousand men altogether. He, however, fought the battle of **Chippewa,** and was obliged to retreat, taking up his position at "Lundy's Lane." In the meantime the enemy spread over the country, and plundered and burnt the buildings of the Canadians, and destroyed the village of St. David's. These acts so enraged the people that they attacked the marauders, whenever they had an opportunity, and scarcely a party returned to its camp without leaving some killed or wounded behind.

26. As soon as General Drummond heard of the invasion, and of the battle of Chippewa, he hastened from Kingston, and arrived at Fort Niagara on the 24th. With eight hundred men he hurried forward to aid Riall, who had begun to retreat. But General

Drummond changed the order, and pushed on and reached the summit of the hill where Riall's camp had been, just as the Americans were within six hundred yards of it. And now took place the battle of **Lundy's Lane**, the bloodiest conflict of the whole war. It commenced at five o'clock in the afternoon and lasted until midnight, when the Americans withdrew, having lost twelve hundred men. The loss of the British was nine hundred, including General Riall, who was taken prisoner while being carried off the field wounded.

27. General Drummond pursued the enemy and besieged them in **Fort Erie**. The latter held the fort until the 5th of November, when they blew it up, and retired across the river. In the west the British still held Mackinaw, although efforts were made to take it from them.

28. During July and August, Sir John Sherbrooke of Nova Scotia, invaded **Maine**, and subdued the State from the Penobscot River to New Brunswick. The British held it till the close of the war.

29. During those three years of Canada's invasion, England had not been able to send out any troops to help her faithful colonies. She had been fighting Napoleon, and in this year had succeeded in having him banished to the island of Elba. This permitted her to send to Canada sixteen thousand soldiers, who arrived at Quebec in September. Sir George Prevost led eleven thousand of these against **Plattsburg**, but his bad generalship made his expedition a failure, on account of which many of his officers felt so ashamed that they broke their swords in vexation, declaring they would never serve again.

30. On the Atlantic sea-board, **Washington**, the capital of the United States, was sacked by the British, but they were afterwards defeated at the battle of **New Orleans** on the 8th of January, 1815. Two weeks before this occurred, on the 24th of December, 1814, the **Treaty of Ghent** had been signed. By it peace was restored to Canada, and the Americans received back the forts and territory taken from them during the war. The blessing of the God of peace upon the loyal resistance of Canada's defenders preserved to this young nation its liberty and its laws.

CHAPTER XI.

UPPER AND LOWER CANADA AFTER THE WAR.

1. Reaction.
2. Army-bills redeemed.
3. Social condition.
4. Cholera.
5. Governors of Lower Canada.
6. Governors of Upper Canada.
7. Exclusion of Americans.
8. Schools—Steamboat.
9. Clergy Reserves.
10. House prorogued.
11. Social condition.
12. Canada Trade Act.
13. Ottawa founded.
14. Sir John Colborne.
15. Toronto a city.
16. Fifty-seven Rectories.
17. Sir Francis Head.
18. Commercial crisis.
19. Census.

1. After war there always happens what is called a **reaction**. It takes some time for the people to resume their former steady habits of work. Some are altogether ruined in this respect for the duties of peace. Thus it was in Canada, but not so much so as in the case of older countries. One reason was, that in a new country every person must either work or starve; another reason was, the causes and nature of the late war. It had been forced upon Canadians; it was one of defence of their homes, their wives, and their children; a war that was cruel in every respect, and from which every generous heart revolted. There was none of the pomp and display about Canada's little forces, that there is about the large armies of older lands, so that the people saw the true character of war, and were glad when they could return to their peaceful employments.

2. Although Sir George Prevost had not shown any of the qualities of a good general, he had endeared himself to the inhabitants of Lower Canada in his civil capacity as Governor. He was recalled to England early in the year 1815, and Sir Gordon Drummond took charge of the province. Parliament granted small **pensions** to those who had been disabled in the war, and also gave presents or gratuities to the widows and orphans of the men who had died while fighting for their country, which, though young, was not ungrateful, and endeavored as far as it was able, to express its sympathy for those who had been brave and loyal. The paper money issued during the contest was also redeemed, that is, the army-bills were called in and their value paid in coin.

Mark the **contrast** between the United States and Canada from the effects of the war. In the United States their own paper money was received by the Americans with distrust, and they were not able to redeem it till long after it was due, and when it had lost a great deal of its value. But in Canada the "Army-bills" passed for their face-value, and were redeemed at once upon the conclusion of the war.

3. In 1816, Sir George Coape Sherbrooke was promoted from being Governor of Nova Scotia, to be Governor-General of Canada. His first care was to relieve the **famine** in the country, consequent upon the failure of the wheat crop. Large sums of money were voted by the Legislature to purchase relief for the sufferers, and money was also lent to the farmers to buy seed grain. But the country was rapidly recovering itself. In the following year the first **banking institutions** were opened in Canada—the Banks of Montreal and Quebec. In 1818, Sherbrooke was succeeded by the Duke of Richmond, but after a short rule of one year he died from the effects of a bite of a tame fox, and was succeeded by Sir Peregrine Maitland, then Governor of the Upper Province. The Earl of Dalhousie became Governor-General in 1820. In the meantime nearly thirteen thousand immigrants arrived in Canada from the Old Country. This influx of population was chiefly owing to the failure of crops in Ireland. These people found ready employment upon the public works, which were now being carried on with energy. The **Lachine Canal** was commenced in 1821, and the **lumber** traffic gave occupation to all hardy men. This trade led to the settlement of the Upper Ottawa, at the same time that it was the cause of a large commerce with England, which in its turn promoted ship-building at Quebec, and two very large vessels, but very little less in size than the "Great Eastern," were built at the island of Orleans, and sailed for England with cargoes of timber.

4. In 1825, McGill College was made a University. Thus the country continued to progress in population, wealth, and education. Nothing could stop its growth, not even the increasing jealousy of the two races of the inhabitants, nor the strife kept up in the Parliament, where a very clever man, by the name of Papineau, was the leader of those discontented with the Government. We

shall talk of the reasons of this discontent in the next chapter. A great calamity, however, afflicted both provinces in the years 1832 and 1834, when the **cholera** spread with alarming violence through all the large cities and towns.

5. The remaining Governors of Lower Canada up to 1837, were Sir James Kempt, appointed in 1828, Lord Aylmer in 1830, Earl G sford in 1835, and Sir John Colborne in 1837.

6. During the war, the civil as well as military affairs of the western province were directed by Sir Isaac Brock, as President, and, after his fall at Queenston Heights, by Sir Roger H. Sheaffe, in a similar capacity, and next by Baron de Rottenburg. In 1813, Sir Gordon Drummond became Lieutenant-Governor, but when he was removed to Lower Canada in 1815, the Hon. Francis Gore was a second time appointed to the helm of state in Upper Canada. In the interim, however, before his arrival in September, the government was administered by Sir George Murray and Sir F. Robinson. In this year Parliament passed a vote of £1,700 for the erection of a monument to the memory of Brock, at Queenston Heights. Efforts were also made **to induce settlers** to take up their residence in the country. Immigrants of good character from the Old Country were offered a free passage and a grant of one hundred acres of land, while a similar grant was to be given to their sons on coming of age. They were also to receive support until their first harvest, and to obtain their farming implements at half price. As a security for good faith, they were required to make a deposit of £10, to be returned upon their fulfilling the conditions of settlement. As one result of these efforts the county of Lanark was largely taken up by immigrants from Scotland.

7. But these offers did not include Americans. The country had just passed through a fiery trial, the people could not forget the vacant seats in the family circle, and the Government thought that Canada would be preserved in its British privileges and freedom, only by making exclusive laws against the Americans. The result was, that the immigration of these people was discouraged, the Government refusing to grant them lands, or even to permit them to take the oath of allegiance, so that they were placed under the ban of the "Alien Act," and were liable at any time to be expelled from the Province. As public feeling became

more calm and considerate, this law fell into disuse, and many Americans, preferring Canada, settled here and became British subjects.

8. An Act was passed in 1816 to establish common **schools**, and the sum of £6,000 was granted to assist in the payment of teachers, and for the purchase of books. A vote of £1,000 was expended in bounties for the cultivation of hemp. During this year the steamboat "Frontenac" was launched on the Bay of Quinté, to run from Kingston to Toronto.

9. The Act of 1791 set apart the **Clergy Reserves**. In Upper Canada these Reserves amounted to two million, five hundred thousand acres, being one-seventh of the lands in the Province. As the country began to be thickly settled, **three objections** were made against continuing the Reserves for the purpose for which they had been set apart. The *first* objection arose from the way in which the Executive Council wished to apply the revenues arising from these lands. The Constitutional Act said they were to be applied to "maintaining the Protestant religion in Canada," and the Executive Council interpreted this to mean that they should be used only to support the Church of England, which in the Mother Country is established by law. But the other Protestant denominations asserted that it was unfair to make this distinction, and that all Protestant churches ought to share alike. The *second* objection was that the grant of so much land in a new country was too large, while the *third* referred to the way in which the Reserves were selected. These two and a half millions of acres did not lie together in a block, but when the early surveys were made, *every seventh lot* was reserved, and as these lots were not cleared for years, the people complained that they prevented the formation of connected settlements, necessary for making and keeping roads in repair. Besides the Clergy Reserves, the Government retained what were called **Crown lands**, which consisted of seven lots in every two concessions, three in one and four in the other, so that these reservations made the settlements very much scattered.

10. The House of Assembly, which represented the people, thought there was justice in these complaints, and commenced to discuss them in the session of 1817. But the Executive and

Legislative Councils, which were in favor of the Clergy Reserves, became alarmed, and persuaded the Governor to prorogue the Parliament. This action was very unfortunate, for it only produced angry feelings, and instead of stopping the agitation against the Reserves, prolonged it for thirty-seven years.

11. Sir Peregrine Maitland became Governor in 1818. In the following year the Hon. W. H. Merritt projected the **Welland Canal** between Lakes Erie and Ontario, and obtained assistance from Lower Canada to the amount of £25,000. In 1820, the population of the Province was nearly one hundred and twenty thousand, and the House of Assembly was increased to almost double its former number of members. The Bank of Upper Canada was started in this year.

12. About this time Upper Canada began to claim from the Lower Province a **larger share** of the importation duties, although the original share of one-eighth had been increased to one-fifth. She also claimed that Lower Canada was in **arrears** to her to the amount of £30,000. This subject of dispute was referred to the Home Government, which took into consideration other matters of trouble between the two provinces. The English Parliament passed a bill called the **Canada Trade Act**, which came into force in 1823. This Act compelled Lower Canada to pay the £30,000, and prevented her imposing new duties on imported goods, without the consent of the Upper Province, or of the Sovereign. The Home Government also advised the two Canadas to form a union; but though Upper Canada was favorable to the idea, it was not at all agreeable to the people of the Lower Province.

13. Although Upper Canada had political troubles somewhat similar to those of Lower Canada, her prosperity was **steadily advancing**. The construction of canals and other public works gave employment to numbers of mechanics, and caused an increased circulation of money, while the cost of living was not so great as at the present time. Steamboats passed to and fro upon the lakes and rivers, and numerous schooners carried on a freight traffic of great profit. On account of the rapids, the navigation of the St. Lawrence was still performed by means of Durham boats or bateaux, which, leaving Kingston, passed the rapids, and after

discharging their freight, were generally sold at Montreal or Quebec, as the labor of going against the current rendered the return voyage profitless. This was not destined to last much longer, for even then the building of the St. Lawrence canals was being thought of. In 1826, the village of **Bytown** was commenced by Colonel By, who was sent out from England to superintend the construction of the Rideau Canal. Bytown has since become the city of **Ottawa**, the capital of the Dominion of Canada. There was also a large business carried on in the lumber trade, but the practice of smuggling robbed the Government of much of its revenue from that source. In the operations of farming there were none of the time-saving machines of the present day, and some of the implements used were of a very rude kind. Schools sprang up all over the land, and although surrounded by many disadvantages, they performed a noble work in the young country. The Province was not without several newspapers, but their circulation was very limited.

14. The year 1827 was marked by the founding of King's College at York. Its name has since been changed to that of the University of Toronto. In this year Sir P. Maitland was removed to Nova Scotia, and Sir John Colborne took his place in Upper Canada. Sir John was a veteran soldier, and had made himself an honorable name, by his unswerving adherence to whatever he thought to be his duty. He was a man of few words, and had a curt way of replying to the many addresses or petitions presented to him. At one time, making a tour through the Province, his uniform answer to addresses of congratulation was, "I receive your address with much satisfaction, and I thank you for your congratulations." And in 1830, when the House of Assembly presented him with a petition full of grievances, he simply replied, "Gentlemen of the House of Assembly, I thank you for your address." The Governor was, however, the right man in the right place during these early days of Canada. Party spirit was very high at this time in both provinces, and sharp words were said which often threatened to lead to riot; but both parties feared the cool, stern man of few words, who was at the head of the Government.

15. Up to 1834, the capital of Upper Canada was known by the name of York, but in this year the town was made a city, and its

name changed to **Toronto**. Mr. W. Lyon Mackenzie was elected its first Mayor. He was also a member of the House of Assembly, and took an active part against the doings of the Executive Council, which made him popular with a large section of the country. But he made many enemies by his sarcastic speeches both in Parliament and out of it, as well as by his stinging writings in his newspaper, the *Colonial Advocate*.

16. The Clergy Reserves still formed the great source of contention between the Assembly on the one side, and the Upper House and Executive Council on the other. The latter, with the Governor, determined to prevent these lands being turned aside from their original use, and for that purpose quietly formed **fifty-seven rectories** of the Church of England, and provided for their support from the Clergy Reserves. This act caused a good deal of excitement, especially in Toronto ; but the Governor had done nothing but what the Act of 1791 permitted him to do. He was soon after recalled from Upper Canada, and Sir Francis Bond Head became Governor in 1836.

17. Sir Francis was just the opposite of Sir John in character and action. While the latter thought to manage parties and parliaments by saying little and acting promptly, the former hoped to control events and overcome all difficulty by his fine oratory, while he neglected proper caution. At any other time he might have made a brilliant and popular ruler, but at this time his course of action only hastened on that crisis which ended in "Rebellion." He had been sent out with instructions to arrange the difficulties in the Province, but on his arrival was induced to disobey his orders, and so only increased the discontent.

18. During the summer of 1837 a severe **commercial crisis** swept over the United States. A seeming prosperity, which had been increasing for some years, suddenly ceased. Merchants became insolvent ; the banks refused to pay coin, and even refused to pay their own notes. The two provinces were affected by this crisis, and in Lower Canada the banks followed the example of those in the United States; but in Upper Canada they pursued a different course, redeemed their notes, contracted their business, and boldly met the "hard times." Sir Francis at once assembled Parliament, to take into consideration the condition of the country,

and although many advised that their banks should pursue the same course as those in Lower Canada, the Governor thought not, and the House supporting his view of the matter, allowed the banks to continue as they had begun. The storm was weathered, and the good name of the Province maintained.

19. The population of Upper Canada was, at this time, about three hundred and ninety thousand. During the year, letters passed between Papineau and Mackenzie, and both continued their appeals to the people to throw off their allegiance to Great Britain and seek **independence.** They found much sympathy for their scheme, although the greater part of the people sided with loyalty and order.

CHAPTER XII.

CANADIAN REBELLION AND PATRIOT WAR.

1. Causes of Rebellion.
2. Executive Council.
3. Canadian and English Parliaments contrasted.
4. Control of Revenue.
5. Arbitrary action.
6. Other Provinces.
7. Responsible Government desired.
8. Rebellion leaders.
9. Lower Canada.
10. Toronto attacked.
11. Navy Island.
12. The "Caroline."
13. Mild winter.
14. Trials.
15. The Wind-mill affair.
16. Courts-martial.
17. End of Rebellion.

1. In order to learn the **causes** of the Rebellion, it is necessary to trace the working of the Constitutional Act of 1791. We have spoken of some of the effects of the clause which set apart the Clergy Reserves. Let us see what were the results flowing from the selection of the Executive Council in the way recommended by the Act, and from the House of Assembly not having control of the revenues from customs duties and the sale of Crown lands.

2. By the Act of 1791, the Executive Council appointed to advise the Governor was to be chosen by the King, that is, by his representative, the Governor. It thus became independent of the House of Assembly, for the latter, representing the people, might wish to pass certain laws which the Council might advise the Governor not to sanction, and even to do the opposite of that

which the country wished. This form of Executive Council was given to all the provinces when parliaments were first introduced into them.

3. It must be remembered that the Provincial parliaments were formed after the general model of that of England. The **House of Assembly** was elective, like the House of Commons, and as there are no peers in the colonies as in the Old Country, the **Legislative Council** appointed by the Crown bore the nearest resemblance that could be, to the House of Lords. The **Executive Council**, to advise the Governor, stood in the place of the Privy Council, which advises the monarch of England. But there was this difference, that the Cabinet of the Privy Council was mostly chosen from the House of Commons, and could be changed, or was obliged to resign its executive functions, if it did not give advice in accordance with the views of the representatives of the people in the Commons. If the King at any time wished to retain a Cabinet in defiance of the Commons, the latter could compel the King and his advisers to yield, because all the money required for the government of the country had to be voted each year by the Commons, and unless this annual vote was passed, the Government could not be carried on. Therefore, the King's advisers would be obliged, in the end, to submit to the people's representatives. A similar power was not given to the colonies in the first place, because it was thought that, in a scanty population, there was not a sufficient number of men qualified for such an important position.

4. Again, you have seen that the English Government **levied the duties** on the imports into Canada, owing to the fear of English merchants that the provinces might put on too high duties. The Assemblies could only tax themselves for money necessary for bridges, roads, and such public works. They had no control over the money or revenue arising from the duties put upon goods coming into the country. The Governor and his Council in each province kept possession of this, which gave them a power that made them independent of the Assembly, so long as the expenses of the Government did not exceed these revenues. They also had the keeping and use of the money arising from the sale of timber and wild lands, called "Crown lands," because the Government claimed the right over all lands not surveyed and regularly settled.

5. As already said, the form of the Executive Councils had been established, because it was thought the best under the circumstances, and if the men who composed them had felt their true position, that they were placed in their high offices, not because they were to have these things for themselves, but in trust for the monarch and the people, there would have been none of the trouble and quarrels which afterwards arose. But having no account to render of their actions, they began, after a time, to do as they pleased, and instead of studying the wishes of the country, we find them often advising the Governor to a course which could not help but stir up angry and obstinate feelings in the Assemblies. The Legislative Councils were also found to side more frequently with the former than with the latter.

6. This state of things existed not only in the two Canadas, but also in New Brunswick and Nova Scotia. In the latter province, and in Upper Canada, all the chief offices of Government became filled by the members of a few families in each province, so that each was said to be ruled by a **family compact**. The chief complaints made by the Assemblies were, that judges were members of the Councils; that the Crown lands were managed or sold so as to favor friends; that public offices were given in the same way, and in Lower Canada, that Roman Catholics were excluded from places of trust.

7. A strong feeling grew up that some check should be put upon the Executive Councils, and the only check possible was to make them **responsible** to the Houses of Assembly, and to give the latter the control of all the revenue. All the means were used by both parties, that had already been employed previous to the passing of the Act of 1791, but the Executive Councils had a great deal of influence, and the struggle went on for many years before the Assemblies gained the victory.

8. In Nova Scotia and New Brunswick the struggle was more quiet and reasonable, but in Upper and Lower Canada some extreme men were led astray by their intense feelings against the men in power, and went so far as to take up arms to overthrow the Government, and rule the country after their own plan. This crisis was called the **Rebellion**, and occurred during the years 1837 and 1838. Rebellion is a very great offence against law and

order, and all nations and people are agreed that it should be punished very severely, with death or imprisonment, and the confiscation of all property. Rebellion constitutes the crime called **high treason**. Notwithstanding these great penalties against such conduct, there were men bold enough to attempt to do by arms what they had not patience to allow to be done by the Home Government. In Upper Canada **William Lyon Mackenzie** agitated rebellion, and in Lower Canada **Louis Papineau** and **Dr. Wolfred Nelson**.

9. In **Lower Canada**, a riot occurred in Montreal on the 6th of November, 1837. Warrants were issued for the arrest of the leaders, but they escaped, and began to excite outbreaks in several parts of the Province. Sir John Colborne sent troops to the different places, and quelled the insurrection at once. This first attempt was put down by the 17th of December, when Sir John returned to Montreal. On the 29th of May, **Lord Durham** arrived at Quebec, as Governor-General. He was empowered to inquire into all the causes of disturbance, and subsequently made a very able report upon the state of all the provinces. He suggested that all the **British American colonies** should be joined in a **union**, or if that were not thought possible just then, that the **two Canadas** should be united. We shall see how these suggestions were carried out. In the meantime, in order to pacify the rebellious portion of the people, he proclaimed a **general pardon** on the 28th of June, 1838, the day on which Queen Victoria was crowned monarch of Great Britain and its dependencies. But rebellion was not yet at an end, for on the very day, the 3rd of November, on which Lord Durham took his departure for England, a second rising took place in the district of Montreal. In seven days, however, this also was put down by Sir John Colborne. As the merciful action of the Governor-General had been so badly returned, nothing was left but to make an example of those who had engaged in this second attempt. **Martial law** was put in force, and after a short but fair trial, at which none but direct proof was taken against the prisoners, twelve were executed, and others banished from the country.

10. In the **Western Province**, after the troops had been withdrawn to Lower Canada, the rebels became bold, and began

to carry out plans which had been formed for some time. They hoped to take possession of the government buildings in Toronto, and set up their own rule at once, and for this purpose collected in large numbers at a place called Montgomery's tavern, about four miles north of the city, during the first week of December, 1837. But there was no perfect agreement among the leaders, and this gave the loyal people of Toronto time to prepare themselves. The Governor sent out a flag of truce to learn what the rebels wanted. The reply was "independence," and that an answer must be returned within an hour. They were told that their demand could not be complied with. That night they marched down towards the city, but were driven back. The next day the Don bridge was set on fire and the Montreal mail captured. In the meantime loyal men had flocked to Toronto, and on the morning of the same day **Colonel McNab** went against the rebels, who numbered about six hundred, and soon put them to flight.

11. Mackenzie, after many adventures, escaped to the United States, and obtained the sympathy of many people there, who formed themselves into societies called "Hunters' Lodges," and subscribed nearly $300,000 to help Mackenzie and his friends, who now called themselves **Patriots**. These took possession of **Navy Island**, about two miles above the Falls of Niagara, where they formed the headquarters of the "Patriot Army." They soon had a thousand men, and some cannon taken from an American fort, and their flag bore two stars to represent the two Canadas.

12. A gathering of rebels took place near London, but dispersed as soon as Colonel McNab went against them. This active officer next formed a camp on the Canadian shore opposite Navy Island, to watch the rebels and prevent their plundering the country. These had the service of an American steamer, the "Caroline," to carry their supplies. Colonel McNab sent a party of men under Lieutenant Drew to capture this boat and bring it to the Canadian shore. It was taken, but the current was too strong to bring it across, and it was set afire and allowed to go over the Falls. The Americans made a great deal of fuss about this act, for they said it was an American boat, and on their side of the river; but they had no right to allow their people to assist the rebels against a country at peace with themselves. The British Government

conferred the honor of knighthood upon Colonel McNab, while the Assembly of Upper Canada passed a vote of thanks to him and Lieutenant Drew, and presented each with a sword, on account of their gallant conduct.

13. The winter of 1838 was very mild, and during January boats were able to run on Lake Ontario and the St. Lawrence, so that Sir John Colborne sent troops from Lower Canada by water. On the 14th of January the "Patriots" were obliged to leave Navy Island, but during February bands of them threatened the Canadian side of the Detroit River.

14. In March, Sir George Arthur became Lieutenant-Governor. This was the most serious time of the rebellion. There were some fears of another war with the United States, on account of two things—the capture of the "Caroline," and the **Maine boundary line.** Troops arrived from England, and the militia were called out. The jails in the large towns were filled with prisoners. Trials now took place. Two prisoners were executed at Toronto, some were sent to the Penitentiary, but the most of them were dismissed to their homes.

15. During the summer, parties of "Patriots" made raids across the frontier for the purpose of plunder. In November, an old **windmill** near Prescott was taken possession of by a large party from the United States. They fortified themselves here for several days, when they were obliged to surrender after forty of their number had been killed. On the 4th of December, four hundred and fifty rebels crossed the Detroit River and took Windsor, but they also were obliged to leave after losing many in killed and prisoners. The most of those taken in these incursions were Americans.

16. In the spring of 1839, **courts-martial** were commenced in Kingston and London, when one hundred and eighty were brought to trial, and condemned to be hanged. But some of these were permitted to return home on account of their youth, and the sentence of others was changed to transportation to Van Diemen's Land. Ten were executed at Kingston for the attack at the "Windmill," while three suffered the same penalty at London for sharing in the "Windsor" affair. Many of those banished died abroad, and after several years the survivors were released and

allowed to return home. The same indulgence was extended to Mackenzie, Papineau, Nelson, and other leaders, who lived to repent their rashness, and to try and atone for it by more useful services.

17. Thus ended the "Canadian Rebellion," and the "Patriot War," which had only delayed reform in the constitution, besides adding all the evils consequent on civil war, and creating mutual distrust among the people themselves.

CHAPTER XIII.

THE PROVINCE OF CANADA.

1. Union of 1841.
2. Terms of Union.
3. Governor-General.
4. Colleges.
5. Municipal system.
6. Changes by death.
7. Ashburton Treaty.
8. Schools—Dr. Ryerson.
9. Sympathy.
10. Immigration—Pestilence.
11. Rebellion Losses Bill.
12. Social condition.
13. Public debt.

1. While the last scenes of the rebellion were being enacted, Lord Durham's report had been printed in England, and copies of it had reached Canada. The project of **Union** with the other provinces was freely discussed, and met with much favor in the House of Assembly in Upper Canada, but was voted down by the Upper House, which seemed unwilling to give up its old privileges. The scheme, however, met with great favor among the people, and the British Government sent out the Honorable Charles P. Thompson, in 1839, to bring about a union between the two Canadas. This gentleman succeeded Sir John Colborne as Governor-General, while the latter returned to England, and was rewarded for his services in Canada by being created a peer, with the title of Lord Seaton. The Parliaments of Upper and Lower Canada now readily assented to a Union, and a bill to sanction the Acts of the Canadian Legislature was submitted to the English Commons. It passed both Lords and Commons, and received the assent of Her Majesty on the 23rd of July, 1840; but, owing to a suspending clause, it did not come into operation until the 10th of February, 1841, when it became law by proclamation.

2. This bill provided for the Union of the two provinces under the name of the **Province of Canada**, with one Legislative Council and one Legislative Assembly. The members of the former were not to be fewer than twenty, to be appointed by the Crown for life; those of the lower house were to be elective, forty-two being sent by each province. The sum of £75,000 was to be granted annually for the working expenses of Government, and the **control** of all the **revenues** was granted to the Assembly. By this clause the judges became independent. The Executive Council was to be composed of eight members, who should be **responsible** to the Assembly. Thus all the ends for which the Assemblies had fought in past years were now attained, with the exception of an elective Legislative Council.

3. During the summer of 1840, the Governor-General visited Nova Scotia and New Brunswick, and met with a warm and loyal reception. For the judicious manner in which he had brought the Canadas to consent to the union, he was raised to the peerage, with the title of Baron Sydenham of Kent and Toronto.

4. In this year, Queen's College, Kingston, was founded, and Victoria College, at Cobourg, became a University.

5. Under the new order of things, **Kingston** was selected as the seat of government, or **Capital** of the "Province of Canada." There Lord Sydenham took up his residence, and there the new Parliament met on the 13th of June, 1841, and was opened with more than ordinary ceremony. The first Executive Council or **Ministry**, as it was now called, consisted of Messrs. Sullivan, Baldwin, Daly, Dunn, Day, Draper, Harrison, and Ogden. One of the most important Acts of this Parliament was the founding of the present **Municipal System**, by which each township, county, town, village, and city manages its own local affairs, and has power to levy taxes for local improvements and local government. Before the Union all such matters were controlled by the Quarter Sessions or Boards of Commissioners.

6. On the 19th of September, the Governor-General died from the effects of a fall from his horse, and the news was received with deep grief throughout Canada. Sir Richard Jackson administered the Government until the arrival of Sir Charles Bagot, in 1842.

7. During this year, the famous **Ashburton Treaty** was made between the United States and England. It received its name from the fact that Lord Ashburton was the principal negotiator on the part of Great Britain, while Mr. Daniel Webster acted for the United States. This treaty settled the dispute regarding the **boundary line** between Maine and New Brunswick. The dispute was about twelve thousand square miles of territory lying between the State and the Province. The treaty gave seven thousand to the United States, while the balance fell to the share of Great Britain. It also fixed the **forty-fifth parallel of latitude** as far as the St. Lawrence, and from that point traced the **dividing line** up the river and through the great lakes, as far as the Lake of the Woods. By it, also, Rouse's Point on Lake Champlain was given up to the United States. The tenth article of the treaty formed the ground, upon which the **extradition** of criminals was first made between Canada and the American Government. This article stipulated, "that each party, upon requisition from the other, shall deliver up to justice persons charged with the crime of murder, assault with intent to murder, piracy, arson, robbery, or forgery upon sufficient proof of their guilt."

8. Sir Charles Bagot died in 1843, and was succeeded by Sir Charles Metcalfe. In the following year the **seat of government** was changed to Montreal. The task of remodelling the **school system** of the Western Province was entrusted to the **Rev. Dr. Ryerson**, who was appointed Chief Superintendent of Education for Upper Canada. After travelling through several countries of Europe and the United States, and acquiring all the practical knowledge possible on the subject, he laid the basis of the system of Public and High School Education for which the Province has since become noted, and which gives every child a privilege that cannot be too highly prized. For thirty years after, he continued his duties in this relation, supported by the good opinion and aid of a generous people.

9. In 1845, the city of Quebec was devastated by two large fires, and twenty-four thousand people were deprived of their homes. To relieve their distress the large sum of £100,000 sterling was subscribed in England, while Canada gave £35,000 currency, in addition.

10. Lord Metcalfe was obliged to resign his position on account of ill health, and the Earl of Cathcart directed the Government until the arrival of Lord Elgin in 1847. When the latter met Parliament he announced the removal of the **duties** in favor of British manufactures, which the Home Government had been in the habit of imposing on Canadian imports, since Canada became a British province. He also recommended the project of a **railway** between Halifax and Quebec. Owing to famine in Scotland and Ireland, some seventy thousand immigrants arrived in the country. Having been crowded in the vessels which brought them over, fever and pestilence broke out among them, and the contagion spread through all the frontier towns. The provinces did all that could be done for the sufferers, and "relief funds" were opened, to which all subscribed without distinction of creed, party, or race.

11. The **St. Lawrence canals** were completed in 1848. For three years an agitation had been going on in Parliament with regard to losses suffered during the Rebellion. The discussion of this question excited all the warmest passions of party. The ministry proposed to pay the losses in the Upper Province by the fund arising from "tavern and other licenses." The French Canadian members would agree to this only upon condition that similar losses in Lower Canada were also compensated. Accordingly a measure was introduced to use the "Marriage License Fund" for this purpose. When the **Rebellion Losses Bill** came up again in 1849, the opposition to it was renewed stronger than ever. Meetings were held throughout the country, and the excitement was intense. But the bill passed both Houses and only waited the assent of the Governor-General. On the 26th of April he gave his assent, and the bill became an Act of Parliament, and a law. No sooner was this known than disgraceful **riots** occurred in Toronto and Montreal. In the latter city the crowd assailed the Legislature while in session, drove out the members and set fire to the building, destroying the valuable library of the House. On account of these things, and the insults which he received, Lord Elgin tendered his resignation, but the Queen would not accept it, and said she approved of what he had done. After a time public feeling subsided, and with more sober and better thoughts the people now sent addresses of sympathy and esteem to the Governor-General. These riots caused the removal

of the seat of government from Montreal altogether. For the remaining two years it was to be held at Toronto, and after that alternately at Quebec and Toronto every four years.

12. The year 1851 was marked by three matters of great importance. The Canadian Government received the transfer of the Post Office Department from the British Government, and a **uniform rate of postage**—three pence per half ounce—was established, while the use of postage stamps was also introduced. Education took a step forward when Lord Elgin laid the corner-stone of the **Normal School** buildings in Toronto, where teachers might receive a special training for their special work. Trinity College was also founded in the same city. During this year also, the first **World's Exhibition** was held in London, England, where the industrial products of Canada were well represented.

13. **Canada was growing rapidly**, and constantly increasing her trade relations with the United States and Great Britain. Each change she had experienced in her government had been suitable to the time when made, and had served to help not only in developing the resources of the provinces, but also in gradually educating the people to rely upon themselves and assume their own government. As Canada had been one of the first to apply steam to the navigation of her lakes and rivers, so now she was not behindhand in commencing the building of railways. In 1851, the Northern and Great Western lines were under construction, and in 1852, Parliament granted aid to the building of the Grand Trunk. In the latter year an Act was also passed establishing what was called a **Municipal Loan Fund**, from which municipalities might borrow money for making local improvements, such as roads, bridges, and other public works. Two years later this Act was extended so as to include Lower Canada. The object of the Act was good, but sufficient checks were not imposed, and many of the municipalities incurred heavy debts upon which they could not even pay the interest, and which had therefore to be borne by the Government. This state of things, and the railway policy of the country, which was far in advance of the times, helped to form a large **public debt;** and in a few years the revenue was not sufficient to pay the expenses of government.

CHAPTER XIV.

THE PROVINCE OF CANADA—(*Continued*).

1. Reciprocity Treaty.
2. Seigniorial Tenure Act.
3. Clergy Reserves settled.
4. Crimean War.
5. Legislative Council elective.
6. Ottawa the capital.
7. Atlantic Cable.
8. Prince of Wales.
9. Census.
10. American Civ'l War.
11. Union Convention.
12, 13. Fenians.
14. Trade relations.
15. Confederation.
16. Dominion Day.

Under Elgin's regime,

1. The year 1854 was marked by three important Acts of legislation. The first was the conclusion of a **Reciprocity Treaty** with the United States. It was to continue for ten years, after which time it could be terminated by either of the parties to it giving one year's notice. It provided for the mutual exchange of, or trade in, numerous articles, the **natural products** of the farm, forest, and the mine—free of duty. It permitted the Americans the use of the St. Lawrence and other Canadian canals, in exchange for the concession to Canada of the right to sail through Lake Michigan. The people of the New England States were also allowed the privilege of the in-shore **fisheries** of the Gulf of St. Lawrence, under certain restrictions. This treaty came into operation in March of the following year, and furnished the **first instance** of Great Britain recognizing the right of her colonies to assist in the negotiations of a treaty where their interests were involved.

2. The second work of Parliament was the **Seigniorial Tenure Act**, which was earnestly demanded by the French Canadian section of the House. The difficulties in connection with this question arose out of the peculiar privileges granted to the seigniors under the old French rule, which privileges had been confirmed to their possessors in 1763 and in 1791, and had greatly interfered with the improvement of the condition of the small farmers of the Lower Province. It thus retarded very much the general prosperity of the country. There had been a protracted agitation for the purchase of the seigniorial rights from the holders of them, and it was now determined to do this according to the

THE PROVINCE OF CANADA. 83

value put upon them by a commission which was to be appointed. Each tenant or small farmer was to pay a certain amount to the seignior, the balance of the price to be paid by a fund granted by Parliament. The sum granted amounted to $2,600,000.

3. The third Act of this session was the final settlement of the **Clergy Reserves** question. It was enacted that the fund arising from the sale of those lands was to be handed over to the different municipalities, to be applied either for purposes of education or for local improvements, as each thought most proper. But such portions of the Reserves as were already in the possession of incumbents were to form a small permanent endowment for the clergy of the churches who held possession.

4. During this year England and France united in an alliance with Turkey against Russia. The scene of the war was the peninsula of the **Crimea**, in the Black Sea. The victory at the Alma, October 17th, furnished an opportunity for both Houses of the Canadian Legislature to forward congratulations to England, along with two drafts of £10,000 each, for the relief of the widows and orphans of the soldiers and sailors of England and France, slain in the contest. This war was brought to a close in favor of the Allies by the fall of Sebastopol, in September of the following year.

5. In December, 1854, Sir Edmund Head succeeded Lord Elgin as Governor-General. An amendment to the Militia Act, which was passed that session, led to the formation of the first regular corps of **volunteers**. The session of 1856 made the Legislative Council elective. Its members at the time, who had all been appointed by the Crown, were to retain their seats during life, but twelve new members were to be elected every two years, and after election to hold their seats for a period of eight years. In order to give effect to this measure, the united provinces were divided into forty-eight electoral districts.

6. The practice of changing the place of Parliament every four years was found to be a source of great expense and trouble, and in the following year a resolution was passed asking Her Majesty to be pleased to select a Canadian city, suitably situated, to become a **permanent seat** for the Government. Within a year it was announced that the Queen had selected **Ottawa** as the capital of

the Canadas. As several of the older cities had hoped to obtain this honor, much disappointment was at first felt, but the wisdom of the choice soon quieted all ill-feeling.

7. During 1858, the **decimal system** of money was substituted for the old Halifax currency of pounds, shillings, and pence, which had been in use up to this time. In August the **Atlantic cable** was successfully laid between Ireland and Newfoundland, and the Queen and the President of the United States exchanged messages of congratulation. What a change since the time when it took four months for news to pass and repass across the Atlantic !

8. Meanwhile the **Victoria Bridge**, which spans the river at Montreal, was being rapidly finished, and the Parliament of 1859 voted a second address to the Queen, respectfully inviting her to visit Canada and perform the ceremony of opening the bridge for traffic. During the session of 1860 a despatch was received, expressing the regret of Her Majesty at not being able to accept the invitation given in the previous year, but intimating that His Royal Highness, the **Prince of Wales**, would visit the country and represent our Gracious Sovereign. This royal visit was made during the months of July, August and September. Commencing with St. John's, Newfoundland, the Prince rapidly visited all the chief towns and cities of the Maritime Provinces and the Canadas. On the 25th of August he opened the Victoria Bridge, and on the 1st of September laid the corner-stone of the present Parliament buildings at Ottawa. Extensive preparations had been made for his reception throughout the length and breadth of British North America. Large sums of money were spent by the various places, and the Canadian heart was kept in a flutter of loyalty by a generous striving to testify due regard for the eldest son of our Queen. It is not necessary to detail all the expressions of loyalty and unbounded attachment felt by British colonists towards his royal mother and himself, which greeted the Prince at every step of his progress through the provinces. After leaving Canada he visited several places in the United States, and was as enthusiastically received there. He returned to England in October.

9. In order to form some idea of the growth of the Canadas during the twenty years of the Union, let us look at the census returns during that time :

```
Census of 1841.—Upper Canada  ............    465,000
   "       "   —Lower Canada  ............    691,000
   "     1851.—Upper Canada  ............    952,000
   "       "   —Lower Canada  ............    890,000
   "     1861.—Upper Canada  ............  1,396,000
   "       "   —Lower Canada  ............  1,111,000
```

This larger increase in the population of the Upper Province over that of the Lower originated in the former a desire, that its interests should have a more proportionate representation than the Union had secured. This feeling was paving the way for a **Union of all the Provinces**, a scheme which was now discussed from time to time both in England and Canada. In October, 1861, Lord Monck succeeded Sir Edmund Head as Governor-General.

10. In the meantime, the **civil war** between the Northern and Southern States had broken out, and had a great influence upon the British provinces. In the first place, there was danger of war at one time, on account of the Americans taking two Southern commissioners from the British ship "Trent," while on her way to England. But they were surrendered again, and the danger passed by. Again, this war caused much money to flow into Canada, where live stock of all descriptions was readily purchased by American dealers at good prices. Wages were also high, and the farmer, the mechanic, and the merchant were enjoying great prosperity. The civil strife lasted until 1865, and during this and the preceding years Canada had much trouble from the lawless men, who came into our land as quiet visitors, and then formed themselves into bands to make **raids** across the border into the United States for the purpose of plunder.

11. In 1864, Lord Monck communicated with the Lieutenant-Governors of the other provinces in regard to a union, and the result was, that a **convention** of thirty-three representatives met at Quebec, in order to take the question of Union into consideration. A union was agreed to, and seventy-two resolutions passed, which were to be submitted to the several Parliaments and to Great Britain. In the following year the Legislatures of the Canadas, Nova Scotia, and New Brunswick adopted the scheme, but Newfoundland and Prince Edward Island left it for further consideration.

12. For several years societies had been forming in Ireland and the United States, called **Fenian Brotherhoods**. These

societies declared themselves enemies of English power wherever it might be, but especially in Ireland, which they vowed to separate from Great Britain. The Fenians in the United States had avowed their intention of invading Canada, and at the close of the civil war purchased at a small cost large quantities of arms and ammunition for this purpose. Disbanded soldiers joined their ranks, and they succeeded in creating a large organization, which was supported chiefly by the lowest class of people, by those who had nothing to lose, and those who felt no respect for order and good government. During the spring of 1866, rumors reached Canada of an intended invasion, and the volunteers were put in readiness for any emergency. On the 1st of June, a body of Fenians, twelve hundred strong, crossed from Black Rock near Buffalo, and took possession of the ruins of Fort Erie, and the Railway depot. They were led by an ex-officer of the American army, named "General" O'Neil. They marched towards the Welland Canal, and took up a position at a place called **Ridgeway**. Here they were met by some nine hundred volunteers from Hamilton and Toronto, commanded by Colonel Booker. A sharp engagement took place, and, although the volunteers were forced to retire, the Fenians received such a check that they were obliged to retreat to Fort Erie. The loss of the volunteers was one officer, Ensign McEachren, and six men killed, and four officers and nineteen men wounded. As the Fenians were left in possession of the field, they were enabled to bury their dead, so that their actual loss was never known. At Fort Erie they were met by seventy volunteers under Colonel Dennis, and lost five killed and several wounded. On the 3rd of June they withdrew to the American shore. Those taken prisoners in Canada were sent to the Toronto jail.

13. This raid created a wonderful excitement in Canada, and corps of eager volunteers were rapidly moved to different points on our extended frontier. Many Canadians scattered throughout the United States left their business and started in companies for their native land, ready to share in its defence. Bands of Fenians assembled at different places near our borders in Lower Canada, but the American Government had commenced to do its duty, and its own troops dispersed the marauders, and arrested their leaders.

The trial of the prisoners captured in Canada took place in Toronto during October, when several of them were condemned to be hanged; but, through the clemency of Her Majesty, this sentence was changed to imprisonment in the penitentiary. Short as the disturbance had been, the country had been put to a great deal of expense and annoyance; but all this was as nothing in comparison with the indignation at, and mourning felt throughout Canada for, the death of the gallant few who fell at Ridgeway. A **monument** has since been raised to their memory in the Queen's Park, Toronto.

14. In 1866, the Reciprocity Treaty between Canada and the United States expired, by lapse of time, and has never since been renewed. The American Government refused to form a new treaty, because it thought Canada had got into such a habit of commercial connection with the Republic, that without a treaty she would be obliged to join the union, and become one of the States. But this action of the Americans only effected a contrary result, for while it was damaging to themselves, it has led Canada to extend her commercial enterprise to other countries, with a consequent benefit.

15. The first meeting of Parliament in the new buildings at Ottawa was on the 8th of June of this year. The ministry introduced resolutions which embodied the remaining steps necessary to complete the work aimed at by the **Confederation of the Provinces.** They were passed by large majorities, and the House adjourned on the 18th of August. Delegates from the provinces now proceeded to England to finally arrange the terms of Union. On the 7th of February, 1867, the Bill for Confederation was brought before the British Parliament, under the title of **The British North America Act, 1867.** It passed both Commons and Lords without delay, and received the royal assent on the 28th of the month. On the following day, "The Canadian Railway Loan Act" was also passed, whereby a loan of £3,000,000 sterling was to be guaranteed for the building of the Intercolonial Railway, in order to connect the Maritime Provinces with the two Canadas. It was carried by a very large majority.

16. The **first of July** of this year (1867) was appointed by Royal Proclamation, as the commencement of this new era in the **history of our** country.

CHAPTER XV.

THE OTHER PROVINCES.

1. Mutual interest.
2. Newfoundland.
3. Nova Scotia.
4. New Brunswick.
5. Prince Edward Island.
6. The North-West.
7. The Pacific coast.

1. The several provinces did not take any real interest in one another until about 1864. Previous to that time each was content to look after its own affairs, and the fact of their having similar systems of government lent a character of sameness to the history of each, which did not awaken in the mass of the people of one province any great curiosity with regard to the progress of the others. Whatever had been said about union before 1864, was said by only a few far-seeing governors, and a few patriotic public men of the colonies. But when in 1867, the union of the four leading provinces was completed, a mutual interest was created, and unity begat sympathy. Let us, then, before speaking of the "Dominion," review the leading events in the story of each of the other British provinces which lie east and west of the "Canadas."

2. **Newfoundland.**—This island was visited in 1575, by Martin Frobisher. In 1583, Sir Humphrey Gilbert took possession of it in the name of Queen Elizabeth, and two years afterwards Sir Francis Drake visited its rocky shores. Sir George Calvert, the first Lord Baltimore, founded its first English colony in 1622, and four years from that time, the French began a settlement at Placentia, which in 1634, paid the English a tribute of five per cent. for the privilege of fishing. In 1654, another English settlement was formed by Sir David Kirke. In 1696, the French obtained the chief control in the island, but in the next year, the "Treaty of Ryswick" restored it to the English. During "Queen Anne's War" the French again obtained the ascendancy, and retained it until 1713, when the "Treaty of Utrecht" gave back Newfoundland and its coast to the British, with the exception of the little islands of St. Pierre and Miquelon, and the right to French fishermen in perpetuity, to fish on certain portions of the

Newfoundland coast, and land for the purpose of curing their fish. In 1762, its capital, St. John's, was captured by the French, but retaken by the English. The famous navigator, Captain Cook, took part in this expedition, and in 1767, he surveyed the coasts of the island. In 1763, the Labrador coasts and Magdalen Islands were joined to Newfoundland, but in 1773 they were restored to Canada. Latterly, however, Labrador has been united politically with Newfoundland. In 1800, a conspiracy to overthrow the Government was discovered by the Roman Catholic Bishop O'Donnell. In recognition of this loyal action, the King conferred upon the Bishop an annual pension of £50 sterling. Newfoundland, from its earliest discovery, has been of great importance on account of its vast fisheries, but its cold climate, and foggy, rocky coasts, have prevented its rapid growth in population. It was accorded responsible government in 1855. The Government consists of a Governor appointed by the Crown, an Executive Council, a Legislative Council, and an Assembly. In 1858, the first Atlantic cable was laid between its shore and that of Ireland.

3. **Nova Scotia.**—Under French rule, this province, along with what is now New Brunswick, was termed Acadia. Its settlements then were few, small and scattered, the chief one being at Port Royal, which was founded in 1605, and another at the mouth of the St. John River. The French settlers devoted themselves to hunting and fishing, and tilled only the more fertile portions of the land. Acadia was taken several times by the English, and as often restored to the French. In 1614, Samuel Argall, with three ships from the English settlements in Virginia, appeared before Port Royal, and after destroying the place, sailed away. But on the strength of this expedition, and of the early voyages of Cabot and Gilbert, England laid claim to Acadia; and in 1624, granted it to Sir William Alexander, by whom the country was named Nova Scotia. In the meantime, however, the French resumed possession of Port Royal, and formed other small settlements along the coasts, so that the English under Sir David Kirke were again obliged to take possession of it by force in 1628. It was restored to France in 1632, by the treaty of St. Germain-en-Laye. It was next captured by the British in 1654, when Cromwell ruled England, but the treaty of Breda, in 1667, gave it back to France.

In 1690, Sir William Phipps destroyed the fortifications of Port Royal, and in 1710, General Nicholson took it for the last time, and changed its name to Annapolis in honor of Queen Anne. The Treaty of Utrecht, in 1713, confirmed England's claim to the country. In 1749, the city of Halifax was founded. The Acadians were expelled in 1755. The final capture of Cape Breton, with its strong fortress of Louisbourg, in 1758, assured future safety and peace to the new province of Nova Scotia. From this time until 1784, Nova Scotia, Cape Breton, Prince Edward Island, and New Brunswick formed one province. They were then separated, but Cape Breton was again joined to Nova Scotia in 1819. Nova Scotia was governed, at first, by the English general commanding in the colony. Afterwards a council was appointed to assist him, and, in 1758, it received a constitution from England. This provided for a joint Executive and Legislative Council, named by the Crown, and an Assembly elected by the people. During the Revolution in the United States, much sympathy was expressed in Nova Scotia for the rebels, so much so that the members for disloyal counties were not allowed to take their seats in the Assembly. After the war, about twenty thousand U. E. Loyalists settled in the Province. In 1814, Nova Scotia granted ten thousand dollars to aid those who suffered by the war in Canada. In 1820, measures were taken to protect the coast fisheries. In 1838, the Executive and Legislative Councils were separated, and ten years afterwards responsible government was introduced. The "Reciprocity Treaty" of 1854 contained clauses, which regu'ated the fishery difficulties between the United States and British America. Up to the time of Confederation, Nova Scotia made great progress, as was shown by its lines of railways, and a system of schools and colleges which is generously supported by the Government.

4. **New Brunswick.**—This province was called the county of Sunbury when it formed a part of Nova Scotia, but, in 1784, it was made into a separate government similar to that of its older neighbor. Fredericton became its capital, and its first governor was Thomas Carleton, under whom it prospered greatly. From 1804 until 1817 it was governed by presidents. In 1809, the British Parliament laid a tax upon timber imported into the United Kingdom from the Baltic, but allowed timber from New

Brunswick to be admitted free of duty. The result was a great benefit in starting the timber trade of the young province. The population was largely increased by the influx of U. E. Loyalists after the Revolutionary war, and, again after the war of 1812-14, when many disbanded soldiers received land-grants in the province. During the hot summer of 1825 extensive fires raged through the forests of the country; six thousand square miles were desolated, and five hundred lives lost. In 1837, the city of St. John was visited by fire, and one hundred and fifteen houses burnt. In the same year, the revenues of the province were given over to the control of the local Government. In 1842, the "Ashburton Treaty" settled the harassing dispute about the "Maine Boundary Line," by dividing the land between the Province and Maine. New Brunswick, with the great resources of her soil, her mines, and her forests, has rapidly overtaken her older sisters, and, like them, can point to her railways and her schools as evidence of advancement.

5. **Prince Edward Island.**—Champlain gave this island the name of St. John. The English claimed it in 1745, when they took Louisbourg, but the "Treaty of Aix-la-Chapelle" restored it to France three years afterwards. Lord Amherst took possession of it again, in 1758, and, in 1763, it was confirmed to England by the same treaty which secured the cession of Canada. In 1767, the island was surveyed into townships of 20,000 acres each, and these again into lots, which were distributed by lottery among the officers of the army and navy by the governor, Lord Campbell. Certain conditions were imposed upon settlers, and they were obliged to pay a quit-rent in lieu of taxes. Thus the tenure of land was not *freehold*, but *leasehold*. In 1797, the rents paid were not sufficient to meet the expenses of government, and the province soon got into debt, and had to be assisted by the Home Government. In 1800, its name was changed to Prince Edward Island, in honor of the Duke of Kent, the father of Her Majesty Queen Victoria. In 1803, through the efforts of the Earl of Selkirk, the population was increased by the immigration of hardy settlers from the Highlands of Scotland. A separate government was given the island in 1770, and, three years afterwards, it received a constitution modelled after that of the other provinces.

This form of government was retained until 1851, when responsible government was accorded. Prince Edward Island has steadily prospered, and shown an activity which has enabled it to keep pace with the larger provinces.

6. The North-West.—This large region of country, stretching away to the west and north of the older provinces of Canada, remained in its primitive condition long after the other provinces began to be settled. Its vast forests, and extensive plains watered by large rivers and lakes, formed a fitting dwelling-place for the native hunter. Its distance from the sea-board delayed its settlement, and for many years the only white men who visited it were the active and brave French traders, who followed the courses of the rivers and trafficked with the natives for furs. Both France and England claimed the country—the former, because it lay near her colony on the St. Lawrence; the latter because her explorers had visited and examined the shores of that great inland sea, Hudson Bay, which took its name from Henry Hudson, who made his first voyage thither in 1610. By the "Treaty of St. Germain-en-Laye," in 1632, the English resigned the whole territory to France, but, in 1670, Charles II., disregarding the treaty, granted to an English company a charter which gave them full control of that extensive country for two hundred years. This company was called the "Hudson Bay Company." Its traders had numberless contentions with the French until after the cession of Canada, and even then its troubles did not cease, for the "North-West Company of Canada" was formed in 1784, and a rivalry sprang up which often led to serious broils. In 1811, the same Earl of Selkirk who had taken such an interest in Prince Edward Island, secured a large tract of land from the Hudson Bay Company, and founded a settlement at Red River. The little colony suffered severely from the quarrels of the companies, and frequently had its property destroyed, and many of its settlers killed. In 1816, troops had to be sent from Quebec in order to restore quiet. In 1821, the strife was ended by the union of the two companies. In 1867, the population comprised, besides Indians, about 10,000 people, who were distributed among the several settlements, or employed by the Company at its forts. The government also was in the hands of the Company.

7. **The Pacific Coast.**—In 1778, Captain Cook explored the Pacific Coast as far north as Nootka Sound. In 1792, Captain Vancouver was sent out by England to arrange certain difficulties with Spain, regarding territory along the coast. He gave his name to Vancouver Island. In 1793, Sir Alexander Mackenzie, a member of the North-West Company, crossed the Rocky Mountains to the Pacific Ocean, and discovered the Fraser River. He also discovered the great river which bears his name. In 1843, the Hudson Bay Company took possession of Vancouver Island, and founded Victoria. In 1844, the boundary line between British Columbia and the United States was defined. In 1859, gold was discovered on the Fraser River. In the same year Vancouver Island and British Columbia became distinct colonies under one governor, James Douglas, C.B. In 1858-'9, Captain Palliser surveyed a route for a Pacific railway. In 1863, the Queen named New Westminster, on the mainland, as the capital of British Columbia.

CHAPTER XVI.

THE DOMINION OF CANADA.

1. British North America Act.
2. Duties of Governor-General.
3. The Senate.
4. The House of Commons.
5. The Provincial Legislatures.
6. Admission of other Provinces.
7. Duties of Parliament.
8. Debt and revenue.
9. Dominion Day.
10. Nova Scotia dissatisfied.
11. Manitoba.
12. British Columbia.
13. Washington Treaty.
14. Changes in Ontario Ministry.

1. The **Dominion of Canada** began in 1867 with the union of the four provinces, of Upper Canada, Lower Canada, Nova Scotia, and New Brunswick. By the "British North America Act" the name of Upper Canada was changed to **Ontario**, and that of Lower Canada to **Quebec**. It is important to understand this Act, because it made provision for three important things : first, how the Dominion was to be governed ; second, how each province was to be governed, and third, how the Dominion might, in the future, be enlarged by adding other provinces.

2. According to that Act, the authority of the **Sovereign** of the British Empire was to be represented by a Governor-General,

in whom was to be vested the power by which the laws are to be carried out. For this reason he appoints the Lieutenant-Governors of the provinces, and the judges of the various courts. He is the commander-in-chief of all the military and naval forces in the Dominion, and no Act of Parliament can become law until he has given his assent to it. In him resides the power to commute the sentence of a court of justice. His responsible advisers were to consist of thirteen members of Parliament who possessed the confidence of Parliament.

3. The **Senate** of the Dominion was to consist of seventy-two Senators appointed by the Crown for life, namely, twenty-four for Ontario, twenty-four for Quebec, and twenty-four for the Maritime Provinces. A Senator must be a British subject, a resident of the Province for which he is appointed, and an owner of property to the value of $4,000 over and above his debts. The Speaker of the Senate is appointed by the Governor-General.

4. The **House of Commons** was to be made up of one hundred and eighty-one members, namely, eighty-two for Ontario, sixty-five for Quebec, nineteen for Nova Scotia, and fifteen for New Brunswick. The number of sixty-five for Quebec was to remain fixed, and form a standard number in proportion to which, and to the increase in population of the several provinces, compared with that of Quebec at each taking of the census, the numbers from the other provinces might be adjusted. A member must be a British subject. He must own property worth $2,500. (This clause was removed in 1874.) This House elects its own Speaker, and in no case can a Parliament continue in existence for a longer term than five years. We see, then, that the Government of the Dominion consists of the Governor-General, the Senate, and the House of Commons.

5. Each province was to have a Lieutenant-Governor, and a Legislature consisting of one or two branches, according to its choice. All the provinces, except Ontario, chose to have two branches, an Assembly elected by the people, and a Legislative Council named by the Crown. Ontario chose to have only an Assembly, which consisted at first of eighty-two members. In all the provinces the Assemblies are elected for four years. Each of the Lieutenant-Governors is aided by an Executive Council or

Ministry, responsible to the Legislature, and through it to the Province, for all measures and Acts of Government.

6. Two steps are necessary to the admission of any other province to the Dominion. (1) The Legislature of that province and the Dominion Parliament must both, by addresses to the Queen, set forth plainly the terms of the proposed union. (2) Her Majesty must sanction the act of union.

7. This **Confederation** of the provinces did not take from them the great boon of responsible government, but only secured it to all in a more complete form. To the Government at Ottawa was given the charge of those matters which concerned all the provinces, such as trade and commerce, the postal service, the taking of the census, the military and naval defence of the country, navigation, the fisheries, coinage, banking and the issue of paper-money, the Indians, criminal law, and the penitentiaries. The duties of each provincial legislature included the levying of direct taxation within the Province, borrowing money on the credit of the Province, the regulation of municipal institutions, licenses, local public works, property and civil rights in the Province, the administration of justice, and education.

8. Each of the provinces had a public debt of its own, but at the union the Dominion became liable for such debts. The provinces also gave up their public revenues to the central government at Ottawa; in lieu thereof, the latter was to pay each local Government a fixed yearly sum to defray its expenses. It was agreed, moreover, that an **Intercolonial Railway** should be built, joining the Maritime Provinces with those in the interior.

9. While the first "Dominion Day" was observed with rejoicing throughout the country, at Ottawa **Lord Monck** took the oath as first Governor-General of the Dominion of Canada. He then, in the name of the Queen, bestowed various imperial honors upon the public men who had been foremost in bringing about Confederation. Sir John A. Macdonald was directed to form a Ministry, and thus became the first **Premier** of the Dominion. Sir N. F. Belleau was appointed Lieutenant-Governor for Quebec, and General Doyle for Nova Scotia. The government of the other two provinces was administered by military officers until the

following year, when the Hon. W. P. Howland, C.B., became Lieutenant-Governor of Ontario, and the Hon. Judge Wilmot of New Brunswick.

10. The elections were held during the summer, and within a few months after they had taken place the several legislatures met. The Hon. J. S. Macdonald became Premier of Ontario, and the Hon. Mr. Chauveau of Quebec. The working of the new Constitution gave much satisfaction in all the provinces except Nova Scotia. Before one year had passed, it was found that the share of the Dominion revenue received by that province did not suffice to meet the expenses of its Government. The people at once expressed their displeasure, and sent petitions to England to have their part in Confederation cancelled. But the Home Government refused the petition, and advised a friendly settlement of the causes of complaint. "Better terms" were granted, and the province became contented. In British Columbia, an agitation commenced in favor of joining the Dominion.

11. In 1868, **Lord Lisgar** became Governor-General. This year saw efforts made to obtain the cession of the North-West Territory to Canada. The two hundred years of the Hudson Bay Company's charter were expiring, and two delegates, Sir G. E. Cartier and the Hon. W. Macdougall, C.B., were sent to England to take the necessary steps for securing that territory to Canada. The English Parliament passed the "Rupert's Land Act," by which the Hudson Bay Company was empowered to surrender its territory to the Crown, which, by proclamation, could annex it to the Dominion, so soon as the usual address of request had been passed by the Canadian Parliament. The latter passed a bill containing the request, and granting £300,000 sterling to the Hudson Bay Company in exchange for its rights of possession, but allowing it to retain its trading privileges. Early in the next year surveying parties were sent out to the vicinity of Fort Garry, for the purpose of laying out portions of the country in townships and lots, preparatory to its further settlement. The presence, however, of these parties awakened fears among many of the inhabitants, that they should lose their lands and homes. This and other causes united to arouse feelings hostile to Canada, and to its acquisition of the territory. A large portion of the population armed them-

selves for resistance, and, under two leaders, Louis Riel and M. Lepine, formed a government of their own, and made prisoners of all persons hateful to them. One of these, Thomas Scott, who was much hated by the self-made rulers, was shot in a brutal manner, during March, of 1870. This act caused intense excitement throughout Canada, and especially in Ontario. On the 4th of May the Parliament at Ottawa passed a bill for the annexation of the North-West, and in July it was formally ceded to Canada by the Home Government. In the meantime, a force of twelve hundred men, composed of British regulars and Canadian volunteers, under the command of Colonel (now General, Lord) Wolseley, proceeded to Fort Garry, only to find the rebels scattered and the colony quiet. The "Manitoba Act" passed in 1870 described the limits of the Province of **Manitoba**, and gave it its constitution. This province lies between the ninety-sixth and ninety-ninth lines of longitude, extending east and west one hundred and thirty six miles, and northward from the United States one hundred and four miles. Its constitution provided for a Lieutenant-Governor, an Executive Council, and two Houses of Parliament (originally, but the "upper" house has since been abolished), and permitted it to send two members to the Dominion Senate, and four to the House of Commons. Its representation in the Commons has since been raised to five members. The Hon. Mr. Archibald became Governor. While these events were happening in the west, the Fenians crossed the frontier of the Province of Quebec at Trout River, on the 25th of May, and at Pigeon Hill on the 28th, but were driven back by our volunteers, when their leaders were arrested by the Americans.

12. **British Columbia**, which includes Vancouver Island, was admitted into the Dominion in the early part of 1871. This province is represented at Ottawa by three members in the Senate and six in the House of Commons, and has a constitution similar to that of Manitoba. In connection with its admission it was agreed that the Dominion should construct a "Pacific Railway," reaching from the western limits of Ontario to the Pacific coast of the new province, to be completed in ten years—a condition which was afterwards found impossible, and the time for the construction of the railway was extended.

13. Let us now consider certain difficulties which had been growing up between Canada and Great Britain on the one side, and the United States on the other. The **first** difficulty was about the ownership of the island of San Juan, lying half-way between Vancouver Island and the American shore, and which both England and the United States claimed. The **second** difficulty was concerning the boundary line between the extreme North-West, and Alaska, which had lately been bought from Russia by the United States. The **third** trouble arose out of the desire of the Americans to use the Canadian fisheries, from which they had been debarred since the lapse of the Reciprocity Treaty. The **fourth** cause of the difficulty was the Fenian raids, Canada claiming that the United States should pay the losses occasioned by them. On the other hand, the Americans demanded that England should pay them, for all damage committed during their civil war, by certain vessels bought and fitted out in England by the Southerners. These American demands were called the "**Alabama Claims**," from the name of one of the vessels. In order to try and settle these several difficulties, England and the United States appointed certain of their statesmen to meet at Washington, and see what each country was willing to do. The Premier of Canada, Sir John A. Macdonald, was one of the commissioners for Great Britain. This meeting was held in 1871, and was called a "Joint High Commission." The result of its labors is known as the **Washington Treaty**, which was signed on the 8th of May. By it the "Alabama Claims" were submitted to an arbitration which met at Geneva, Switzerland, in the next year, and which awarded the United States the sum of $15,500,000, in payment of the claims. England promptly forwarded the amount to the American Government. The dispute about the island of San Juan was submitted to the Emperor of Germany, who decided, in December, 1872, in favor of the United States. The boundary line of Alaska was defined by the treaty itself. The clauses in the treaty relating to the fisheries allowed citizens of the United States the use of the British American fisheries for twelve years, in return for the use of their fisheries, the reciprocal admission of fish and fish-oil free of duty, and the payment of a sum equivalent to the excess in value of the British over the American concessions. This

amount was to be fixed by a commission to meet at Halifax for that purpose. The "Fenian Claims" were not mentioned in the Washington Treaty, and Canadians expressed a good deal of ill-feeling about the omission. But Great Britain adjusted the matter with the Dominion, by guaranteeing a loan of £2,500,000 sterling.

14. In December, 1871, the Hon. John Sandfield Macdonald resigned the premiership of Ontario, and was succeeded by the Hon. Edward Blake. The former died in the early part of the following summer, and was much lamented throughout the province.

CHAPTER XVII.

VICE-ROYALTY OF LORD DUFFERIN.

1. Dual representation.
2. New Brunswick School Act.
3. Hon. A. Mackenzie, Premier of the Dominion.
4. Riel and Lepine.
5. Progress in 1876.
6. Commercial depression—St. John fire.
7. Halifax Commission.
8. Tariffs—Revenue and Protective.
9. Sir John A. Macdonald becomes Premier—Lord Dufferin.

1. In June, 1872, Lord Lisgar was succeeded by Lord Dufferin as Governor-General of the Dominion. Thus far, since Confederation, it had been the privilege of members of the Provincial Legislatures to be elected to the Dominion Parliament. This system, which was called "dual representation," was done away with in this year. In consequence of this, during November, the Hon. Edward Blake resigned the office of Premier of Ontario, and was succeeded by the Hon. Oliver Mowat. In March, 1873, the Hon. Mr. Mowat introduced in the Assembly of that province a bill to enable the various municipalities to settle their debts to the Government on account of the Municipal Loan Fund Act of 1852. This bill, which was passed, proposed to cancel the larger portion of these debts, so that the balance might be paid. The Act also accorded a proportionate amount to those counties which had not borrowed at all, or had been faithful in paying off their indebtedness. This Act was a great benefit, and removed many heavy burdens.

2. By the "British North America Act," the subject of education was left to each province. The Legislature of New Brunswick, in 1871, passed an Act in favor of one system of public schools, and excluding "Separate schools." This displeased a large party, which tried to have the Act set aside as contrary to the Act of 1867, and for this purpose sought the aid of the Dominion Government. It, however, declined to interfere. An appeal was made to the Crown in 1873, which confirmed the Act of the New Brunswick Legislature.

3. **Prince Edward Island** was admitted to the union in 1873. Its constitution has this peculiarity, that its Legislative Council is elective. It has four members in the Senate and six in the House of Commons. The course pursued by the Dominion Government with reference to the Pacific Railway up to this time, did not meet the full approval of the House of Commons. Surveys had been made of the several routes proposed, but the work of construction was not yet commenced. Two large companies were striving to obtain the contract for building the road. In the meantime a "general election" had been held for the House of Commons, and when that House met, early in this year, the charge was made against the Government, that it had received money from one of the companies in order to influence the late elections. The inquiry into these grave charges took up a great part of the year, but before Parliament could pass an opinion upon the report of the committee, the pressure upon the ministry became so great that the Premier, Sir John A. Macdonald, was obliged to resign. The Hon. Alexander Mackenzie was then called upon to form a ministry. The new Premier, in order to test public opinion in regard to what had taken place, asked the Governor-General to dissolve Parliament. The request was granted, and another general election held in January, 1874, which resulted in the return of a very large majority for the new ministry.

4. In the session which followed, it was provided that the Pacific Railway should be proceeded with by the Government, and that those portions more necessary for the opening of the North-West should be built first. A law was passed which changed the manner of taking votes at elections. The **ballot** was to take the

place of the old system of "open voting." Louis Riel had been returned for a county in Manitoba, and coming to Ottawa, took the oath of membership of the House of Commons. He was, at the same time, a fugitive from justice, for a "true bill" had already been found against him by the grand jury in his own province, as one of the murderers of Thomas Scott. Riel was thus an outlaw, and debarred from taking his seat in Parliament. A motion was therefore passed expelling him from the House. Riel fled the country. Lepine, however, was tried for the murder of Scott and sentenced to death, but in answer to petitions which were presented for his reprieve, the Governor-General changed the sentence to imprisonment, and subsequent banishment from the country ; and Riel and others were included in the decree of banishment. In this latter year the Hon. John Crawford, Lieutenant-Governor of Ontario, died at Toronto, and was succeeded by the Hon. Donald A. Macdonald.

5. The events of 1876 show further progress. Upon the retirement of the Rev. Dr. Ryerson, as Chief Superintendent of Education for Ontario, it was thought best that this important department should be represented in the Government of the Province. The Hon. Adam Crooks was the first to become Minister of Education. Part of the territory lying near Manitoba was erected into the District of Keewatin, under the Lieutenant-Governor of Manitoba, assisted by a Council. Treaties had previously been made with the Indians of this new country, by which they surrendered their lands, and came under the protection of the Canadian Government. Some three years before, a large force of Mounted Police had been distributed to various points throughout the North-West for the maintenance of order. During the year, the Intercolonial Railway, running along the southern banks of the lower St. Lawrence, and through New Brunswick and Nova Scotia to St. John and Halifax, was completed and open for traffic. But the greatest evidence of the advancement of the Dominion was the display of its products at the **World's Fair**, held this year at Philadelphia, where, one hundred years before, the thirteen colonies had declared their independence. At this exhibition, Ontario excelled the other provinces in her educational department, which was the most admired of all, and received high praise.

6. During the two previous years the Dominion had felt the influence of the commercial depression, which more or less affected the whole world. Like other crises of the kind, it had been caused by the over-trading and extravagance growing out of years of prosperity. But such times have their lessons, and it is to be hoped that our country will be all the wiser for the severe lesson taught. In addition to these troubles, in 1877, New Brunswick suffered severely by the fire which nearly destroyed the city of St. John, causing a loss of millions of dollars and some lives. Sympathy with the sufferers was widely expressed, and contributions of all kinds were forwarded at once, not only from different parts of the Dominion and England, but from several cities of the United States.

7. One of the leading events in our history is the award given in 1878 by the Halifax Commission, appointed under the Washington Treaty, to estimate the difference in value of the American and Canadian concessions, in what are known as the "Fishery Clauses" of that treaty. The award, which was in favor of Canada, amounted to $5,500,000, and was paid during the year.

8. At the general elections in September, a new question was placed before the people for their decision. It was the question of **tariffs**, and as it is one of those issues which, when once brought forward in a country, is likely to recur with each future election, it requires some explanation. That portion of a tariff which relates to the duties on imported goods, may be framed in two ways : *First*, duties on foreign goods may be so arranged that, while sufficient for purposes of revenue, they shall not be so heavy as to keep these goods out of the country. *Secondly*, duties may be so increased that those classes of foreign goods, which may be made in a country, shall be prevented from coming into it, and the people of that country shall thus be induced to manufacture such classes of goods for themselves. A tariff framed for the first purpose is called a **Revenue Tariff**, while one arranged for the second purpose is called a **Protective Tariff**. Up to this time the Canadian tariff had been one chiefly for purposes of revenue, and trade with other countries had been left as free as possible. This state of things the Government of the Hon. Mr. Mackenzie wished to retain. But the Opposition in Parliament, led by Sir

John A. Macdonald, asserted that a more protective tariff would be better for Canada. The two parties, therefore, went before the electors for a decision on this question. The result was the return of a large majority of members for the House of Commons, pledged to a protective tariff.

9. The Hon. Mr. Mackenzie accordingly placed the resignation of his Ministry in the hands of the Governor-General, who at once intrusted to Sir John A. Macdonald the duty of forming a new Government.

Close upon these events came the departure of Lord Dufferin from Canada, after a residence of six years. During that time this nobleman had, by his ability in the duties of his high office, as well as by the active interest he evinced in whatever tended to promote the welfare of the Dominion, secured the esteem and affection of all classes of the people.

CHAPTER XVIII.

VICE-ROYALTY OF LORD LORNE.

1. Lord Lorne, Governor-General.
2. Protective tariff.
3. Dismissal of Lieut.-Governor Letellier — Local elections.
4. New Brunswick—Ontario.
5. Relief for Ireland.
6. Canadian Commissioner to England.
7. Canadian Pacific Railway—Syndicate Terms.
8. Census, 1881.
9. Effects of the census on legislation.
10. Attempt upon the life of the Queen.
11. Dominion Election, 1882; Ontario election, 1883.
12. Departure of Lord Lorne and the Princess Louise.
13. "Constitutional" questions.

1. Her Majesty, the Queen, had been pleased to name her son-in-law, the Marquis of Lorne, to be her representative in the Dominion, in the place of Lord Dufferin. On the 25th of November, 1878, Lord Lorne and his royal consort, the Princess Louise, landed at Halifax, and were greeted in a manner which left no doubt as to the loyal sentiments of the Canadian people. The Governor-General was at once sworn in, and no delay was made in reaching the Capital, except to receive along the entire journey the repeated tokens of a welcome, which was ever heartily accorded His Excellency and the Princess in their future movements through the Dominion.

2. Upon the meeting of Parliament in 1879, the new Ministry proceeded to make good their pledges of a protective tariff. The duties on sugar, woollen and cotton goods, and implements, were raised so as to encourage the production of these articles in Canada. In the meantime the long commercial depression had begun to pass away, business was reviving, and very soon various manufacturing industries commenced to spring up throughout the country.

3. During the preceding year, the affairs of the Province of Quebec had been the subject of much dispute between the two parties in the Commons, and the matter reached a climax in this session. In 1878, while the Hon. Mr. Mackenzie was Prime Minister, Mr. Letellier, the Lieutenant-Governor of Quebec, dismissed the Provincial Ministry. This action was strongly condemned by the Opposition at Ottawa, and when they came into power, the Administration of Sir John A. Macdonald advised the Governor-General to remove the Hon Mr. Letellier from his office. The question was referred to the Home Government, as to whether such removal was permitted by the "British North America Act, 1867." The answer was to the effect, that since the Act said " a lieutenant-governor shall hold office during the pleasure of the Governor-General," and since the general rule was that the Governor-General exercised his powers "by and with the advice of his Ministers," therefore the Home Government declined in this instance to recommend the Governor-General to act contrary to that advice, but hoped that the whole matter would be taken into consideration again. The result, however, was that the Hon. Mr. Letellier was removed. These circumstances excited a great deal of interest, on account of the **two relations** in question,—the relation of a governor to his Ministry—and the relation of a lieutenant-governor to the Governor-General. Under responsible government the events must be very unusual which would warrant a governor, either of a province or of the Dominion, in refusing the advice of his Cabinet ; while the offence should be very grave, indeed, to make it necessary to dismiss a lieutenant-governor from his office. The Ministry of Mr. Joly, which had succeeded the "dismissed" one, was so feebly sustained at the polls this year, that it was soon obliged to resign. In Ontario, Mr. Mowat was returned to power with a large support.

4. The month of February, 1880, was marked by the death of Lieutenant-Governor Chandler of New Brunswick. He was succeeded by the Hon. R. D. Wilmot, who was, at the time of his appointment, Speaker of the Dominion Senate. In the same month that province lost its Parliament buildings by fire, but the sum of $75,000 was immediately voted to restore them. In March, the Hon. George Brown, of Toronto, a foremost statesman and journalist, was shot while sitting in his office, and died the following May. He was a man of great energy, upright purpose, and decided opinions. From 1844, when he established the *Globe* newspaper, until the time of his sad death, he exercised a leading influence upon all questions, which concerned the welfare of the old Canadas and of the Dominion. In June, the Hon. John Beverley Robinson entered upon his duties as Lieutenant-Governor of Ontario.

5. The failure of the crops in Ireland in the past year was the cause of much destitution there, and called for a great deal of assistance, which was cheerfully given. Relief funds were started, to which contributions were sent from all parts of the world. Besides private and other donations, the Canadian people, through their House of Commons, gave $100,000, and the Assembly of Ontario voted $20,000.

6. Two very important topics occupied the attention of the Dominion Parliament in 1880. The first was the creation of the office of a Canadian Commissioner to England, who was to reside in London, and whose duties were to have reference to Canada's intercourse with the Home Government. He was also to look after Canadian interests as regards matters of emigration and commerce. Sir Alexander Galt was made the first Commissioner to England, and sailed in March for the scene of his new duties.

7. The second subject of importance was that which had already been much talked about in the country—the Canadian Pacific Railway. Hitherto its construction had been wholly carried on under contracts let by the Government. In the early session of the year, the Ministry stated that the wild lands of the North-West were sufficient to pay the expenses of building the railway, and a measure was passed, setting apart 100,000,000 acres of those lands for that purpose. During the summer, the Premier, Sir John A.

Macdonald, and the Minister of Railways, Sir Charles Tupper, proceeded to England, and were successful in forming a company, or **Syndicate**, for the purpose of taking the construction of the line out of the hands of the Government. In order to hasten the matter, and relieve the impatience of the country as to the terms of the project, the Ministers returned from England, and Parliament was summoned to meet in December. The **leading terms** of the new contract were, that the Syndicate should build, equip, and operate the road by the 1st of May, 1891. In payment they were to receive $25,000,000 and 25,000,000 acres of land, and to have the privilege of bringing into Canada, free of duty, foreign purchases of materials necessary for the railway and telegraph lines. There was also a provision, that for twenty years no charter should be granted for the building of a competing line in the North-West, south of the through railway. These terms were earnestly discussed during the Christmas recess. When the House re-assembled in January, 1881, a strong Canadian company made an offer to the Government to build the road for $22,000,000 and 22,000,000 acres of land, and without the customs' privileges to be granted to the Syndicate. The Government, however, defended the terms of the former scheme, the bill for which was passed on February 1st, by a majority of seventy-nine. The work of construction was at once commenced, and has since been vigorously pushed forward.

8. The census taken in 1881 showed a large increase in population in the four older provinces of the Confederation, and also gave the number of inhabitants in those provinces admitted into union since the previous census in 1871. The following is a comparison of the figures, as taken at the two periods :

	1871.	1881.	Increase.
Ontario	1,620,851	1,923,228	302,377
Quebec	1,191,516	1,359,027	167,511
New Brunswick	285,594	321,233	35,639
Nova Scotia	387,800	440,572	52,772
Prince Edward Island	....	108,891	
Manitoba	....	65,954	
North-West Territories	....	56,446	
British Columbia	....	49,459	
Total	3,485,761	4,324,810	
Total increase for the Dominion		839,049	

9. In accordance with the provisions of the "British North America Act, 1867," the relations of the provinces to one another are affected, as to the **representation** of each in the House of Commons, by the increase or decrease of population, as shown in the taking of the census every ten years.

10. The Dominion Parliament, in 1882, passed an Act for the purpose of dividing into four districts that portion of the North-West Territory, lying beyond Manitoba and Keewatin. The new districts received the names of Assiniboia, Alberta, Saskatchewan and Athabaska. There was also passed, the **Redistribution Act,** which re-arranged the boundaries of constituencies, for the election of members to the Dominion Parliament. The beginning of the year was marked by the death of Rev. Dr. Ryerson, "the fruit of whose life and works will be felt for good in this province in ages yet to come." In March, the public was startled by the news, that the life of our Queen had been endangered by a pistol bullet fired by a half-crazy man. Happily he missed his aim, but the nervous feeling of anxiety awakened throughout Great Britain and the colonies did not subside for some time.

11. The general election held in June showed the people still in favor of a protective tariff, the Ministry of Sir John A. Macdonald being returned to power with as strong a majority as before. By this election the representation of the provinces in the Commons was as follows : Ontario, ninety-two ; Quebec, sixty-five ; New Brunswick, sixteen ; Nova Scotia, twenty-one ; Prince Edward Island, six ; British Columbia, six ; Manitoba, five.

The elections for the Ontario Assembly in the following February, 1883, again returned the Hon. Mr. Mowat to the position he had held for ten years as the leader of the Provincial Government.

The Hon. G. W. Ross became Minister of Education in the place of the Hon. Adam Crooks, whose health had become completely broken by six years of work and care, in connection with his department. The Hon. A. M. Ross succeeded the Hon. S. C. Wood as Provincial Treasurer.

12. With the early autumn came the close of the *régime* of Lord Lorne, and the regretted departure of himself and the Princess Louise from our shores. Like his predecessors, His Excellency gave untiring attention to the duties of his exalted station.

Accompanied by the Princess, he had visited every province of the Dominion. In 1881, he made the journey of the prairies of the North-West, and in 1882, along with the Princess, went by way of San Francisco, in order to reach our sister province on the Pacific coast. Everywhere they received the evidences of appreciation and hearty good-will.

13. Mention has been made of certain questions of legislation, about which the Provincial parliaments had differed from the Dominion Parliament, and which were referred to the Home Government for decision. Let us see how such reference had been provided for in the Act of Confederation, and how it worked.

Under this Act, the Governor-General-in-Council has the power of **disallowing** any Acts of the Provincial legislatures, which may be thought to be beyond the limit of the "Specified Subjects" for legislation allotted to them by the Act. The exercise of this privilege by the central Government is sometimes disputed by the Provincial governments, when the reason for **disallowance** is not very clear. In such cases, the question of **the right to legislate** may, with the consent of the Province interested, be referred for settlement to the Supreme Court of Canada, established in 1875. It has, moreover, at times, occurred, that one or both of the parties to the question in dispute have desired, in addition to the decree of the Supreme Court, to obtain the opinion or decision of that portion of the Queen's Privy Council in England called the **Judicial Committee,** and permission for an appeal having been granted, questions of the above nature were then referred to that Committee. Such a reference, in these cases of doubt, is the same as asking the Imperial Government to explain the force of its own Acts. Imperial Acts, like that of 1867, form the basis of the Canadian Constitution and cannot be altered, except with the concurrence of the Home Parliament. For this reason, all questions arising under such Imperial Acts, and referred to the Courts for decision, may be called **Constitutional Questions,** and their decision forms "precedents," by which future differences may be more readily settled. Of this character, have been the appeals of Nova Scotia and British Columbia for "better terms," as well as that of the protesting party in New Brunswick regarding her "School Act." **The Provinces of Ontario** and Manitoba have recently made reference to the same authority, for a decision respecting the north-west boundary of the former province. "Precedents" of a somewhat similar nature are also obtained, in instances where the Governor-General hesitates to follow the advice of his Cabinet, and desires, with its sanction, to refer to the Home Government for further instructions, as was the case in the "Letellier affair." Thus we see that the privilege of appeal or reference to the Imperial authorities upon vexed questions, serves a good purpose in assisting to solve difficulties, which could not be foreseen in forming the Act of Union.

CHAPTER XIX.

VICE-ROYALTY OF LORD LANSDOWNE.

1. Lord Lansdowne, Governor-General.
2. A question of privilege.
3. "Oath of office"—Quebec.
4. Public questions.
5. "Temperance" Question.
6. "Separate School" Question.
7. "British Connection."
8. Our volunteers in Egypt.

1. **Lord Lansdowne**, the fifth Governor-General of the Dominion, opened the second session of its fifth Parliament, in January, 1884. The work of this session had especial reference to the railway interests of the country, and to the re-arrangement of the subsidies to the provinces, to meet the necessities of some of them. The Franchise Bill for extending the privilege of voting, was again held over. The measure regarding the **subsidies** provided for the increased claims of the older provinces, and also placed upon a fairer footing with them, those provinces admitted or created since 1871. The Canadian Pacific Railway Syndicate had, in the three years of its existence, pushed forward its great work with such energy that some 1,300 miles were in operation, and had also become possessed of several smaller lines of railway, considered necessary as feeders to its main line. The consequence was, that the company was obliged to appeal to the central Government, not only for relief of terms as to its obligations to the Government, but also to ask a loan of $22,500,000, in order to complete its original contract. The legislation was passed granting aid in both these particulars. The Grand Trunk Railway Company,

which now included the Great Western and Midland Railway systems, also sought and obtained legislation to enable it, among other things, to double-track its line between Toronto and Montreal. Liberal grants were made to assist the various railway enterprises in the several provinces. Under this Act, and that of the subsidies, the Province of Quebec was somewhat relieved from the very heavy burden of a large debt, incurred through the lavish aid she had given for years to the building of provincial railways.

2. During this session there was raised what is called "**a question of privilege.**" It was, whether Sir Charles Tupper, the Minister of Railways, was entitled to retain his office as such Minister and his seat as a member of the Commons. At the close of the session of 1883, Sir Charles had, at the instance of the Cabinet, gone to England and performed the duties of Commissioner in the place of Sir A. T. Galt, whose term had expired. During this service his expenses were to be paid, but he was not to receive the salary of the office, and he returned to Canada in time to be present as Minister in the late session. It was affirmed that in accepting the office, the Minister of Railways had violated the rule of Parliament which obliges any member to resign his seat, who accepts a salaried office under the Crown, and forbids any minister to receive any salary except such as is attached to his department. It was said in defence that the expenses of the office could not be called salary, and that therefore the rule in question had not been violated. The Committee on Privileges and Elections, however, reported to the House that the Minister of Railways had not forfeited his seat. With the close of the session, Sir Charles resigned his seat in the Cabinet and in the House, and was appointed in the usual way to succeed Sir A. T. Galt, as Commissioner to England.

3. The term of office of Lieutenant-Governor Robitaille of Quebec, having expired, the Hon. L. R. Masson was appointed his successor, in November of this year. The latter, however, refused to take the oath of office in the customary form, stating that he could not conscientiously deny the Pope's "authority, ecclesiastical or spiritual, within this realm." The oath was modified in conformity with that formerly permitted under the Act of 1774, in which were omitted the objectionable phrases, and Mr. Masson was sworn in.

*4. Notwithstanding the youth of the Dominion, its history has developed a large number of public questions. Some of these have come down from the previous history of the provinces, some have grown out of the new relations under Confederation, while others have arisen out of the requirements of our own industries, or from our trade relations with Great Britain and foreign countries. Many public questions are such for only a short time. They come up suddenly and are as quickly decided. Others remain before the people for years as subjects of discussion and demanding legislation. In this way they influence the election of the lawmakers of the country, and ask for careful study. Let us note briefly how some of the questions of to-day have **arisen, grown** through agitation, and become more or less **embodied in the laws** of the country.

5. One of these questions is that of **Temperance**—a protest against the manufacture and sale of intoxicating liquors. It began very early in the life of the provinces. By means of *moral suasion* from the pulpit, the platform, and the press, and the formation of *societies* pledged to its principles, it has gained a large following, and procured important legislation restricting the sale of these liquors. After Confederation, the leading societies of the provinces united to form the **Dominion Alliance,** under which the agitation has since been maintained. In Ontario, in 1872, the Crooks Act was passed, which limited the licenses in a municipality in proportion to its population. In 1878, the Dominion Parliament enacted the Canada Temperance Act, better known as the **Scott Act**, because promoted by the Hon. R. W. Scott. This gives municipalities the right, by vote, to prohibit the sale of liquors within their limits. This privilege has received the name of **local option**, and, when passed by any section, is prohibitive of the sale of liquors for three years, when it may be repealed or continued according to the sentiment regarding it. Its adoption by municipalities has been a matter of contest in each instance, while scarcely a session of parliament has passed, in which the Act itself has not been the subject of debate and amendment. In 1883 and 1884, it came into force in a large number of municipalities. On account of the social habits of the people, and of the

---

* See Chapter XXIV. Secs. 10 and 12.

very large amount of money invested in the manufacture and sale of these liquors, the Temperance movement is destined to be an exciting public question for many years.

6. **Separate School Question.** We have read in the foregoing pages of the prompt provision made for education in the early history of the provinces. The Primary or Public Schools especially received the deserved attention and monied support of the legislatures. Owing to the number of religious denominations in the country, and an amiable purpose to prevent any jealousy between them, it was generally thought best to limit the teaching in these schools, to those branches of study which would furnish pupils with the knowledge, necessary to their making their way in life, and becoming intelligent citizens. *Distinctive* religious teaching, as, for instance, that of the catechism or forms of any particular Church, was not provided for, as it was thought that these belonged to the duties of the home and the churches. A further motive for making the Public Schools non-denominational was, that they would be more largely attended, and thus become of a **national** character. The Protestant people of the provinces, although many favored a mixed course of secular and religious teaching, gave up their private opinions to the desire for **one** national system of schools. They were no doubt greatly influenced to this action by the agitation against the Clergy Reserves, during which agitation the stand was taken, that public revenues ought not to be given to the furthering of any particular Church.

The Province of Quebec has, however, taken a different position on this question, for two reasons: because the large majority of the population is of the Roman Catholic Church, and on account of the privileges granted to it in 1763. It is not only a law of that Church, but a matter of conscience with its members, that, in the Primary Schools, their children should be taught the catechism and especial duties enjoined by their Church, along with the secular branches of study. When, therefore, the Union of 1841 gave the two Canadas so many things in common, the Roman Catholic minority of Upper Canada sought to obtain for themselves the privilege enjoyed by their Church in Lower Canada. They pointed to the fact, that the Protestant minority of the Lower Province had a separate class of schools of their own. Upper

Canada being as largely Protestant as Lower Canada was Roman Catholic in population, caused the demand for Separate Schools in Upper Canada to become a very large **Public Question.** The demand for these schools, however, gradually gained ground, so that between 1841 and 1867, many bills were passed increasing their privileges and efficiency. The Confederation Act confirmed the existence of the respective Separate School systems of Ontario and Quebec, as they were at that time. Although the fact of their existence in these two provinces was thus settled in 1867, the **question** is often discussed under various phases. In the **other provinces,** the discussion is, whether the same Act extended the right to establish Separate Schools within their boundaries.

7. Our national relationship to the Mother Country, or **British connection,** as it is called, is the oldest of our public questions, every step in our history having a reference to it. Since 1814, the intercourse of Great Britain and Canada with the United States has grown into close friendship, while their mutual commerce has grown to immense value. But in the face of all this, we have learned that it does not need the chances of unfriendly war, to make our national relationship a public question, for even the conditions of friendly trade and intercourse have done so. Our very nearness to the United States, and the comparison between our commerce with them, and that with Great Britain, has caused "British Connection" to be discussed not only in Canada, but across the "line," and beyond the Atlantic. This was very much the case in 1884, and out of the discussion of the question in England grew the Imperial Federation League, with branches in every section of the Empire, for the purpose of promoting a closer union of all parts of the Empire with its centre. Thus, out of the discussion of Canada's natural place in the Empire, has arisen a still larger "question," which must run its course of time and agitation, until it becomes a matter of immediate importance.

8. This same year (1884) furnished an instance of the Imperial sentiment in the Colonies. Their attention having been drawn to the war, which England was waging in Egypt and the Soudan, native troops from India and volunteers from Australia and Canada went with alacrity, to form parts of the British brigades fighting in

the land of the pyramids and the Nile. Canada furnished a special contingent, composed of men brave, hardy, and experienced in guiding boats over the rapids of our own magnificent rivers. About four hundred men under command of Lieut.-Colonel F. C. Denison, and with Captains Aumond, of Ottawa, and Mackay, of London; Colonel Kennedy, of Winnipeg; Dr. Neilson, of Kingston, and the Rev. Abbé Bouchard, as Chaplain, were brought together in a few weeks, and sailed, on the 15th of April, for Alexandria. There they formed part of the expedition up the Nile to relieve the brave General Gordon, who was besieged in Khartoum by the wild tribes of the desert. Although Khartoum was taken, and General Gordon killed ere the relief could reach him, the arduous work of the volunteers was well done and received the thanks of the British Parliament. The volunteers returned within the next two years.

CHAPTER XX.

NORTH-WEST REBELLION.

1. Causes of the Rebellion.
2. Louis Riel.
3. Duck Lake.
4. Depredations of the rebels.
5. Suppression of the Rebellion—Fish Creek—Batoche.
6. Colonel Otter—Major-General Strange.
7. Trial and punishment of the rebel leaders.
8. Results—Cost—Rewards.
9. "Riel" sympathy in Quebec.
10. Dominion topics.
11. "Issues" at Provincial elections.
12. Chinese question.
13. Colonial and Indian Exhibition.
14. Jubilee year of Her Majesty's reign.
15. Incorporation of the Jesuits.

1. There are times when the discussion of a "public question" may be carried so far as to end in **rebellion**, or armed resistance to government. As already mentioned, the Dominion did not enter at once into peaceable possession of the large territory acquired under the "Rupert's Land Act." There was resistance on the part of the half-breed population, which ceased only when the expedition under Colonel Wolseley reached the banks of the Red River. Then followed the forming of the Province of Manitoba, in 1870. The evils which these people had fancied would happen, did not take place. They were treated kindly, and their houses and farms secured to them. But having once been led into

rebellion, they were ill-at-ease under the new order of things, and as settlers from the eastern provinces came into Manitoba, many of the old inhabitants sold their "land scrip," and removed beyond the limits of the new province, to the unsurveyed lands of the territories. There they settled in villages along its great rivers, and took up the land after the fashion of their former holdings, that is, in narrow farms running back from their villages from one to two miles. Meantime, the Dominion Government had resolved to construct to the Pacific Ocean the railway which was promised in 1871. Under the conditions of the Act of 1880 for that purpose, it was now necessary to survey the territories, in order to know which "sections" should be given to the Railway Company, and which reserved for sale to future settlers. From this it will be seen, that the very same state of things, with regard to these lands, was being prepared, which gave rise to the rebellion of 1869. From time to time, since 1874, those who had "squatted" on these lands asked for "land scrip," such as had been given in Manitoba. The Government refused, for one reason, that many of those now asking had already received Manitoba scrip, which they had sold. Another reason was, that the shape, in which they laid out their claims, would interfere with the survey of the lands as agreed with the Railway Company. As more of the half-breeds came into the territories, and repeated the action and petition of the first-comers, the difficulty was only increased.

2. In 1884, they thought to make a stronger movement. Their leader up to this time had been Gabriel Dumont, a half-breed of much ability, but who could not even read. In order to secure a leader of experience, an invitation was sent to Louis Riel, residing in Montana, and who had led the Rebellion in 1869. His term of banishment having expired, he accepted the invitation and arrived at Batoche in July. He at once prepared a "bill of rights," setting forth the demands of the half-breed cause. The loyal inhabitants now formed themselves into volunteer companies, under the direction of Colonel Irvine of the Mounted Police. Riel's next effort was to seek what he could make out of the movement for himself. He offered the Government to settle the whole difficulty if he were given $35,000, declaring he was "head and front" of the half-breed question. No attention was paid to his

offer, but in January, **1885**, the force of the Mounted Police was increased. Meantime, Riel and Dumont had been smuggling rifles and ammunition from the United States, and had also visited the various bands of Indians to secure their sympathy. On the 17th of March, Riel formed a Provisional Government, making himself President. He now proceeded to seize government stores, and imprison loyal people.

3. In order to meet this stage of open rebellion, Colonel Irvine left Regina with a force of police, to unite with his second officer, Major Crozier, at Prince Albert. The latter, however, thinking he was able to check the rebels, and protect the government property at **Duck Lake**, led out a party of about one hundred police and volunteers. These were met by a larger force of rebels and Indians, and forced to retreat with a loss of twelve killed and several wounded, while the rebels firing from ambush lost but half that number. Swift runners carried the news of this rebel success to the most distant Indian tribes. Many of the Indians left their "reserves," contrary to the terms of their treaty with the Dominion Government, and under several chiefs went to increase Riel's forces, or preyed upon the whites in the vicinity of the reserves.

4. Events now moved **very quickly.** Crozier was defeated on the 26th of March, and on the 29th, at Eagle Hills, the Indians killed two white men, and laid siege to Battleford. Two hundred and ninety miles west of Battleford was Fort Pitt, with nineteen Mounted Police. Twenty miles farther a small settlement existed at Onion Lake, and ten miles beyond Onion Lake was another settlement at Frog Lake. At the latter place, on the 2nd of April, while the people were in church, the Indians took them prisoners, and in answer to the least remonstrance, shot the men, nine in all, including the two priests. Two women were made prisoners, but John Pritchard and three other half-breeds bought their freedom, and conveyed them to safety. On the 13th, the Indians burnt the buildings at Onion Lake, and made prisoners of the settlers. On the 14th, the police left Fort Pitt, and with the inhabitants reached Battleford on the 21st. Crowfoot, a powerful chief of the Blackfeet tribe, remained loyal. The United States sent troops to prevent their Indians from crossing the frontier and joining the rebel Indians.

5. The news of this armed rebellion created great excitement in the Dominion. Parliament was in session at Ottawa, and at once sent Major-General Middleton to take charge of the battalions to be sent to quell the disturbance. The volunteer force of every province furnished its quota promptly. The events in the **suppression** of the rebellion followed each other, as rapidly as those which marked its rise. General Middleton reached Winnipeg on the 27th of March, and was at Clarke's Crossing on the 17th of April, with a force of 950 officers and men. On the 20th of April, Lieut.-Colonel Otter was sent with a strong detachment to Battleford, the centre of a large disturbed district. On the 24th, Riel made a stand at **Fish Creek**, near Batoche, where he had made the best use of the natural features of the country to intrench his force. Here there was sharp skirmishing for thirteen days, when the rebels withdrew to **Batoche**, keeping the volunteers in check until the 12th of May, when the rebel rifle-pits were carried at the charge, and the rebels fled. Riel was captured, and Dumont escaped across the "line."

6. Meanwhile, Colonel Otter with his force was engaged in overawing the disaffected Indians. For nearly two months he moved from point to point, following the bands of Indians to prevent their massing, and seeking to force them back to their reserves, a step necessary in order to protect loyal settlers. His district was extended, the marches long and difficult, but the duty, like that of other detachments, was well carried out. Several lively skirmishes took place with the Indians, the principal of which was at **Cut Knife Creek**, on the 2nd of May. The result was the Indians dispersed, and Chief Poundmaker gave himself up. In **Alberta**, Major-General Strange, with a force organized in the territory, did similar work, maintaining order, and preventing injury to the settlers. He had a skirmish with Chief Big Bear.

7. The **trial** of those taken in rebellion was conducted before Judge Richardson at Regina, the capital of the North-West Territories. Riel was tried for **high treason** in July, and hanged on the 18th of September. Five chiefs and two Indians were executed for the murders committed, and others were sent to prison for various terms.

8. Thus ended the **second Riel Rebellion**, after an active resistance of three months.

Over 5,000 volunteers were in the field during an unfavorable season of the year. The difficulties, of marching and conveying supplies, were beyond the conception of those who remained at home in the older provinces. In the various actions, there were 26 killed and 103 wounded. Others contracted diseases from exposure to climate, fatigue, and hardships to which they were unused. The cost to the Dominion exceeded $5,000,000.

When the troops were withdrawn, the Mounted Police force was further increased. Parliament was yet in session, and recognized the services of the volunteers by votes of thanks, pensions to the disabled, and an Act granting, to every active member of the expedition, 320 acres of land in the Territories. A vote of $20,000 was made to General Middleton, while Her Majesty conferred the honor of knighthood upon him, and the Hon. A. P. Caron, the Minister of Militia.

Confidence was speedily restored regarding the Territories as a safe residence for settlers, and the tide of immigration moved once more to the fine wheat-fields of the North-West.

9. While the affairs at the seat of the late troubles were being reduced to order, much of the excitement incident to them was transferred to the Province of Quebec. There was a sympathy of "race" for Riel, and a large section of the French Canadian people, although quite willing that the rebellion should be quelled, were greatly aroused when it became known that Riel must die, as the punishment of his second act of folly. Mass meetings were held in the cities and towns of the Province. The cry to "avenge Riel" became a political one, and in the Local Legislature and the Dominion Parliament, prominent men supported resolutions of sympathy, which were, however, refused by large majorities.

10. The session of 1885 passed the Dominion **Franchise Act,** which had been carried over several sessions. By it the qualifications of voters at Dominion elections were made uniform.

In the autumn, the Canadian Pacific Railway was **completed** to Port Moody on the western coast. The Company had urged forward the work, and finished it nearly six years sooner than stipulated. Its extent is 3,028 miles from east to west, besides

432 miles of branch lines. In this year also the Hudson Bay was explored, with the view of shortening the route for wheat cargoes to the English market.

As the **Fishery clauses** of the Washington Treaty would expire on the 1st of July of this year, interim legislation was passed, to continue their privileges for that season, in the hope that the United States would agree to a suitable arrangement in behalf of their own fishermen.

11. In 1886, the Hon. J. S. D. Thompson became Minister of Justice, and the Hon. George E. Foster, Minister of Marine and Fisheries.

All the provinces held their **local elections** this year, and returned the existing governments to power, with the exception of Quebec. Each contest was marked by some definite **question** or issue. In **Nova Scotia** the demand for an increased subsidy having been refused by the Dominion Government, the Hon. Mr. Fielding, the provincial Premier, proposed a resolution in the Legislature, which was carried, and which asserted it to be to the advantage of the Province to withdraw from Confederation. As an expression of sympathy with this resolution, the Province returned his Ministry with an increased majority. **Prince Edward Island** was agitating for Dominion aid to construct a tunnel beneath the Northumberland Straits, to connect it with the mainland, and sustained the Government of the Hon. Mr. Sullivan. In **British Columbia**, legislation was very active regarding matters relating to the development of the Province, such as the construction of railroads and docks, the opening up of new gold fields, and the restriction of Chinese immigration, as interfering with white labor. The Ministry of the Hon. Mr. Smithe was returned to power. **Manitoba** supported the Hon. Mr. Norquay as Premier. The Province was desirous of a larger control of public lands, and of reducing the monopoly of the Canadian Pacific Railway, as against the building of competing branch roads. In **Quebec**, the Hon. Mr. Mercier, through the "Riel" cry, had succeeded in forming a "National Party," to promote especially French Canadian interests. He utterly defeated the Ministry of the Hon. Dr. Ross. The latter, however, held office until the meeting of the Legislature in 1887, when he was defeated upon the election of Speaker, and a government led by the Hon. Mr. Mercier succeeded. The elections in **Ontario** were upon the questions of Separate Schools, religious instruction in public schools, temperance, and the franchise. Although Mr. W. R. Meredith, the leader of the Opposition, made a strong fight, the Ministry of the Hon. Mr. Mowat was returned with a large majority.

12. Allusion has been made to the **Chinese** question in British Columbia. The immigration of these people having been very great, the Dominion members for that province had, in 1883 and '84, pressed the Government to pass an Act, which would prohibit the Chinese coming into Canada. This was not complied with, but a motion was passed to restrict and regulate their immigration. When Parliament rose, the Hon. J. A. Chapleau, and Mr. Justice Gray of British Columbia, with Mr. N. F. Davin, M.P., as Secretary, were made a commission to inquire into the whole question. This commission having reported, an Act was passed in 1885 imposing a duty of fifty dollars upon every Chinese coming into Canada, but excepting members of the Chinese Government, consuls, men of science, tourists bearing certificates from their Government, and Chinese wives of white men. The Act also forbade the Chinese in Canada holding any court for the trial of their fellows.

13. On the 4th of May, at London, England, Her Majesty opened the **Colonial and Indian Exhibition.** As its name implies, it represented the peculiar products and varied development of the colonies and dependencies of the Empire. In this feature, it was of vast importance, and of great utility to British subjects all over the world. Canada took a large interest in the exhibition, and often the eye of the visitor to-day will see the diploma of the exhibition, hung in a prominent place in counting-house, factory, and school-room, showing how general and varied was the competition. It was fitting, that His Royal Highness the Prince of Wales acted as the Executive President of the exhibition, for his father, the late Prince Consort, not only projected the idea of a world's exhibition, but labored untiringly to promote the first of the kind—that of 1851. As an evidence of the satisfaction given by the "Colonial and Indian Exhibition," the several colonies contributed to the expense of making the exhibition a permanent one.

14. Early in January, 1887, the House of Commons was dissolved, and S:r John A. Macdonald's Government went to the country. The election took place on the 22nd of February, and resulted in the return of the Government, but with a reduced majority, the "Riel" cry having affected their support, as it had that of the "Bleus," in Quebec. The new House met on the 13th of April, when Sir Charles Tupper, who had resigned his post of High Commissioner, was made Finance Minister. He was elected for Cumberland, Nova Scotia. The cost of the late rebellion and its effect upon the revenue, had produced a deficiency in the latter of nearly $6,000,000. To provide for this amount, the **duties** on imported goods were increased. This necessity gave an opportunity to the leaders of the Opposition in Parliament, Messrs. Blake, Laurier, Mills, and Sir Richard Cartwright, to advocate strongly a policy of "free trade," as in the interests of the country. The **trade question**, in its various features, was often referred to during the session, and brought out the best debating power on both sides of the House. The question of prohibition a'so received a large share of attention.

This being the **jubilee year** of the accession of Queen Victoria to the throne, Parliament voted a humble address to Her Majesty.

15. In Quebec, the Ministry of the Hon. Mr. Mercier introduced and passed an Act, granting incorporation to the Society of Jesus, or Jesuits. The value of immovable property to be held by the Society under the Act was limited to $30,000. Frequent reference has been made to the demands of the provinces for increased subsidies, or "better terms," and to the subjects of legislation, whereon the provinces had appealed to the Home Government against the Dominion. In October of this year, the Premiers of the provinces, excepting British Columbia, with several of the members of their Cabinets, met in a conference to consider the above questions.

In 1888, the Dominion Parliament passed an Act, which removed from the Canadian Pacific Railway Act the monopoly clause, which had prevented charters being granted to new lines of railway, which might compete with that road. The effect in Manitoba was a great activity in projecting new roads.

The session closed on the 22nd of May, after passing an address to Lord Lansdowne, whose term as Governor-General of Canada had expired. He was, however, to proceed to India as viceroy of that large and important dependency of the Crown.

CHAPTER XXI.

VICE-ROYALTY OF LORD STANLEY OF PRESTON.

1. Dominion Ministers.
2. Jesuits' Estates Bill in Quebec Legisl. ture.
3. Jesuits' Estates Bill debate at Ottawa.
4. Sentiment in the country.
5. Separate Schools abolished in Manitoba.
6. Seal-hunting dispute.
7. The McKinley Bill—Commercial Union.
8. The New House.
9. Death of Sir John A. Macdonald.
10. Hon. J. J. C. Abbott, Premier.
11. Public works scandals.

1. In June, 1888, Lord Stanley of Preston arrived in the Dominion, and entered upon his duties, as the representative of the Queen.

Sir Charles Tupper having again been appointed High Commissioner to Great Britain, the Hon. George Foster became Finance Minister, and his place, as Minister of Marine and Fisheries, was conferred upon the Hon. C. H. Tupper, son of the High Commissioner. The Hon. J. G. Haggart was made Postmaster-General, and the Hon. Edgar Dewdney became Minister of the Interior, in the room of the Hon. Thomas White, whose recent death had been deeply regretted by all parties.

Ever since the expiration of the **Washington Treaty**, there had been frequent efforts to bring about an agreement with the United States, in regard to their use of the Canadian fishing-grounds. A treaty had been drawn up which was accepted by our Parliament, but rejected by the United States Senate, although strongly recommended by President Cleveland.

2. It was to Quebec, however, that special attention was drawn this year, on account of the directness with which the Premier, the Hon. Mr. Mercier, undertook to set at rest the question of the **Jesuits' Estates**.

The story of this vexed question dates back to 1759, when General Amherst, at the surrender of French Canada, guaranteed to the inhabitants not only the exercise of their religion, but also the retention of their property. These terms were confirmed in 1763 by the Treaty of Paris. In the course of the previous history of French Canada, several orders of the Roman Catholic Church had established themselves in the country, and received from the King of France large grants of land for the purposes of their mission work. One of these orders, the Society of Jesus, or Jesuits, had acquired over 6,000,000 acres. In 1774, the Society was suppressed by the Pope, while in 1791, George III. cancelled its rights as a corporation, so that its lands were confiscated and became **Crown Lands**. The Church has ever since maintained a protest against this action of the Crown, upon the ground that once bestowed upon an Order of the Church, these lands should have reverted to the latter, when the Order was suppressed. The Crown did not acknowledge this argument, but held possession of the lands, and set them aside for the support of education. When, however, there was at any time an attempt made to sell them, the Church authorities would protest against the sale. Under such circumstances very few sales were made, and the estates brought little or no revenue to the Crown.

In 1888, therefore, Mr. Mercier introduced a bill in the Legislature for the purpose of settling the "question," and enabling his Government to dispose of the lands. The bill granted $400,000 to the Roman Catholic Church for the surrender of its claim to any title in the "estates." At once, there was a protest from the other orders of the Church, that the whole of this compensation should not go to the Jesuits, although the latter claimed it. In order to make the settlement final, it was enacted in the bill that the Pope —the only arbiter accepted by the claimants in affairs relating to their Church—should apportion the amount, and that his receipt should cancel all claims whatever. Of the $400,000, only $160,000 went to the Jesuits, $140,000 were given to the Laval University, and other sums to various missions. At the same time, the bill gave $60,000 to the Protestants of the Province for their educational institutions.

3. It has been noticed that the "Riel" episode gave rise to a **race** cry, and to what was called the "National Party." Under cover of this excitement, Mr. Mercier had seized the opportunity

of carrying through the Jesuits' Estates Bill. It, in its turn, produced a strong feeling among the Protestants of the Dominion, the expression of which feeling received the name of the **religious** cry. As the Provincial Act was subject to disallowance by the Dominion Government, there were those who were prepared to strive for the annulling of the bill. On the 26th of March, 1889, Mr. W. E. O'Brien, member for Muskoka, moved, in the House of Commons, a resolution "condemning the action of the Quebec Legislature in passing the **Jesuits' Estates** Bill, and asking to have it disallowed." The two reasons given were, that it granted public funds to endow religious bodies, and that it recognized a right in the Pope, an alien potentate, to influence legislation in this country. Mr. Dalton McCarthy, Q.C., member for Simcoe, seconded the resolution. It was debated for two days, the bill being defended by members on both sides of the House, especially by the Minister of Justice, Hon. John Thompson, and a leading member of the Opposition, Hon. David Mills, who addressed themselves chiefly to the relation of the bill to the Act of Supremacy. Although the debate did not satisfy everybody in the country, as to the soundness of the argument for the defence, the House decided by a vote of 118 to 13, that the Legislature of Quebec had not exceeded its powers in passing the bill.

4. During the summer, the excitement in the country was in no way abated, and a strong effort was made to induce the Governor-General to disallow the bill, even against the advice of his constitutional advisers. He refused. The sum of the whole matter, therefore was a triumph for Mr. Mercier's Ministry, the settlement of a vexed "real estate" question in the Province of Quebec, and a very uneasy state of feeling in the rest of the Dominion.

In 1889, Sir John Macdonald took over the Department of Railways and Canals, and the Hon. Charles Colby became President of the Council.

5. The session of 1890 served in a great measure, to divert the interest of 1889 from a question of "religion," to one of "race." Mr. Dalton McCarthy moved the second reading of a bill, to do away with the use of French, as an official language in the Legislature of the North-West Territories, which, so long as they are **territories**, are under the tutelage of the Dominion

Parliament. The motion was defeated by a vote of 117 to 63. In **Manitoba,** this year, a bill was passed abolishing *Separate Schools.* Petition was made to Ottawa to veto the Act. The Government refused, in the following year, to do this. Reference was made to the Supreme Court, which gave its opinion in 1891, that the Act was beyond the ability of the Province to pass. The Government of Manitoba then appealed to the Privy Council, which reversed the decision of the Supreme Court of Canada.

A committee was appointed, during the session of 1889, to investigate a charge against General Middleton for appropriating to his own use, during the late rebellion, furs thought to be the property of rebels. The Committee reported, censuring the General, who resigned his post as head of the militia force.

6. In addition to the Fisheries question on our Atlantic coast, this year developed an equally important dispute between Great Britain and Canada on the one side, and the United States on the other, with regard to the right of our vessels to catch seals in the Northern Pacific. The United States claimed, that having purchased Alaska from Russia, it succeeded to Russia's claim to that part of the ocean as a "closed sea." They seized the vessels of **Canadian Sealers** in the season of 1890, which brought matters to a very serious issue.

7. It has been mentioned that when the Reciprocity Treaty expired in 1866, the United States refused to revive the Treaty, in the hope that Canada would seek **Annexation**, that is, form a **political union** with them, rather than lose the freedom of their trade. As already stated, this refusal had a contrary effect. The same party in the United States has since looked for the same desired result, by the enforcement of a very high tariff. This also failed. Acting along the same line of "force," the "Alien Labor Law" was passed, which enacted that those Canadians living along the border, many of whom found ready employment in the States, should not be allowed the privilege of such employment, unless they resided wholly in the United States. A further use of the **Tariff**, as a means of coercion, was made in the year 1890. What is called the **McKinley Bill** was passed, increasing the rates to such an extent as to forbid trade with any countries, which would not comply with conditions irksome to a **free people.**

The consequence was, that the trade hitherto carried on in horses, cattle, barley, and other natural products, fell off very much. This measure has also failed in its aim. Canada at once turned her attention to the **British markets**, and has since sent her natural products there, with the prospect of obtaining as lucrative a market for those articles, as was had before with the United States.

The immediate effect in Canada of the McKinley Bill was a great deal of discussion of how to get over the difficulty, which seemed to threaten us, in losing the United States market. A few proposed to adopt the plan of "Annexation." Others advocated **Commercial Union**, which meant "free trade" between Canada and the United States, but would at the same time compel us to adopt their tariff against all other countries. As their tariff was over forty per cent. higher than that of Canada, "Commercial Union," if adopted, would have cut off the larger part of our trade with Great Britain. Others again desired to have the old Reciprocity Treaty renewed, but as this referred chiefly to "natural products," there could be little hope of its renewal, so long as the United States insisted upon forcing their manufactured goods upon Canada. This was thought to be an injustice to our manufactures, in which money had been invested under the conditions of our own protective tariff, and would mean disaster to very many of our investors.

8. That the people might decide which plan, or policy of the discussion should be adopted by the Government, Sir John Macdonald, as Premier, asked the Governor-General to dissolve Parliament. This was done on the 4th of February, 1891, and a new election held on the 5th of March. The various aspects of the **Trade question** were thoroughly discussed by all parties. The elections decided in favor of maintaining the existing policy of a "protective" tariff, and the Government was returned with a majority of twenty-seven. The new House met on the 29th of April, and elected the Hon. Peter White as Speaker.

The discussions on trade topics and our "National relationship" were continued for some time during the session. The "Annexation" movement was however rejected, for not only the supporters of the Government, but the majority of the Opposition also, threw the weight of their influence against it.

9. The fatigues of the recent election campaign, followed by the heavy work of the session, told severely upon the feeble health of the aged Premier, and after only a week's illness, Sir John Macdonald passed away, on Saturday, the 6th of June.

On Monday following, the announcement of the **death of Sir John Macdonald** was made in Parliament. It was voted that a public funeral should be accorded him, and that Parliament should stand adjourned until the 16th inst. Eloquent addresses of sympathy and eulogy were delivered by members of both sides of the House. The Hon. Mr. Laurier, leader of the Opposition, during his speech, said: "Sir John Macdonald, from the date he entered parliament, is the history of Canada, for he was connected and associated with all the events, all the facts which brought Canada from the position Canada then occupied, to the present state of development which Canada has reached. His actions always displayed a broad patriotism, a devotion to Canada's welfare, Canada's advancement, and Canada's glory."

10. When the House met on the 16th of June, it was made known that the **Hon. J. J. C. Abbott** had been called to the premiership. The remainder of the session lasted until the end of September. There was an extended debate upon **Prohibition**, and a royal commission was appointed to collect information upon the whole question of the liquor traffic and its influence.

11. During the last session of the previous parliament, attention had been drawn by Mr. Barron, member for North Victoria, to certain letters which had appeared in the provincial press of Quebec, charging that the Hon. Thos. McGreevy, member for Quebec city, had for several years received large sums of money, from a firm of contractors engaged in the construction of public works. It was charged also, that those contractors had received information, as to the terms of the tenders of other firms offering for the same public works, and were thus able to underbid the others. It was claimed that this practice had been pursued since 1882. In **relation to these charges,** the Hon. Mr. McGreevy stated in the House that they were false, and Sir Hector Langevin, Minister of Public Works, asserted that he had no knowledge of any such wrong-doing by his department, and demanded that the charges should be investigated. In this session of 1891, the whole

matter was referred to the Select Committee on Privileges and Elections. The Committee finished its work in July, and reported that the charges were proved, and the Minister of Public Works had cognizance of these misdoings, and of the use of the money so obtained, in influencing elections in the Province of Quebec. Sir Hector's resignation of his portfolio was accepted on the 9th of September. On the 29th, the Hon. Thos. McGreevy was expelled from the House of Commons.

CHAPTER XXII.

LORD STANLEY OF PRESTON, GOVERNOR-GENERAL—(*Continued*).

1. Government Scandal in Quebec.
2. Jamaica Exposition — Japan— St. Clair Tunnel.
3. Census of 1891.
4. Sault Ste. Marie Canal.
5. Death of Canadian statesmen.
6. Western Provinces—Schools.
7. Centenary of Ontario.
8. Quebec.
9. Eastern Provinces.
10. Sir John Thompson, Premier.
11. Tariff "Question."
12. Treaty with France.
13. "A Point of Procedure."

1. During the inquiry into these astounding facts, there was discovered an equally bad state of affairs in regard to the **misuse** of **subsidies** voted for the building of railways in the Province of Quebec. The Dominion Senate, therefore, made an order for a Committee to investigate this **second scandal**. This Committee made its report on the 11th of September, showing that members of the Quebec Government had received large sums of money from the railway contractors, as the price of their receiving such contracts.

Following the Senate Committee's report, Lieutenant-Governor Angers appointed a commission of judges to inquire more fully into the charges made against his "Advisers." This commission found the facts confirmed, and that the Premier, the Hon. Mr. Mercier, was guilty of knowledge of these facts. The Lieutenant-Governor thereupon **dismissed** the Mercier Ministry, and called on Mr. de Boucherville to form a ministry. The latter advised the dissolution of the Legislature, which took place on the 22nd of December.

2. So keenly did the country feel the **disgrace** of the shameful scandals brought to light in connection with its public works,

that due interest was not shown at the time in other important events of the year.

The **Jamaica Exposition** was opened on the 27th of January, by Prince George of Wales. Canada, following her policy of exhibiting her products on these occasions, sent as her special commissioner, Mr. Adam Brown, of Hamilton, who spared no means in seeking to promote a trade between Canada and the West Indies. Our flour and dairy products received special attention, being unexcelled.

The **two events**, however, of chief moment to Canada, were supplied by her two great railway companies, each of which this year completed and put into operation, works for the extension of their special traffic. On the 29th of April, the first of the Canadian Pacific Railway's line of steamships on the Pacific Ocean arrived at Vancouver from Yokohama, thus giving Canada direct communication with **Japan** and **China**. On the 19th of September, the Grand Trunk Railway opened for service its **tunnel** beneath the St. Clair River, between Sarnia and Port Huron, thereby making an all-rail connection between its Canadian and United States lines.

3. In the session of 1892, Parliament received the report of the **census** of the Dominion taken the previous year. The total population of Canada was found to be 4,829,411, an increase of only 504,601 in the past ten years. Not only had immigration from Europe failed to increase the population of the Dominion, as expected, but there had been during the decade, a large emigration from Canada to the United States. This was owing to the unusual attractions there of high speculation, and the consequent increase in wages, salaries, and opportunities for "risk" to those who had the ready money to invest. The small increase in our population seemed discouraging to those who esteemed Canada to afford large advantages to thrifty settlers. The Opposition did not fail to make the finding of the census an occasion of attack upon the Ministry, which had held power throughout the period. The "National Policy" and its methods were charged with all the failings of the census, and asserted to have been detrimental to Canada. The Government on its side claimed that the other facts gathered by the census, regarding the condition of the population, and increase of wealth of the country, showed that Canada had made substantial

progress, and that the foundations already laid, had been so built upon as to assure the future good of the country.

The census showed also, that while there was a small total increase, there had been a considerable movement of the population, from one section to another of the Dominion. This fact would require some alteration to be made in the **representation** of the provinces in the Dominion Parliament. This re-arrangement will take effect upon the dissolution of the present parliament, and compared with that of 1881, will stand as follows:

PROVINCES.	HOUSE OF COMMONS. 1881	HOUSE OF COMMONS. 1891	SENATE. 1891
Ontario	92	92	24
Quebec	65	65	24
Nova Scotia	21	20	10
New Brunswick	16	14	10
Manitoba	5	7	4
British Columbia	6	6	3
Prince Edward Island	6	5	4
North-West Territories	4	4	2
	215	213	81

4. All efforts at reciprocity of trade with our neighbors were cut off, by President Harrison's message to Congress, and a bill passed in accordance therewith, to close the **Sault Ste. Marie** canal against Canadians. This Act only taught another lesson along the line of making ourselves independent of United States public works, and our parliament accordingly urged forward the canal on the Canadian side of the river.

5. Death again entered the ranks of our public men this year. The **Hon. Alexander Mackenzie**, who was Premier of the Dominion from 1873 to 1878, and who, in spite of feeble health, had held his seat in the House of Commons ever since, died on the 17th of April.

On the 24th of May, the Lieutenant-Governor of Ontario, Sir Alexander Campbell, passed away. He was one of the **fathers** of Confederation.

In June, British Columbia lost her first minister, the Hon. John Robson, by death. He was in England in the interest of his province when he was stricken down. He had been leader of the Government since 1883. He was succeeded by the Hon. Theo. Davie, Q.C.

6. Since the completion of the Canadian Pacific Railway, the Government of **British Columbia** has been active in opening up its rich mines, and giving communication to them by means of short railways. Gold, silver, and copper are found in abundance, while the province exports coal largely to California. In this year the Hon. Edgar Dewdney was made Lieutenant-Governor.

Manitoba held provincial elections this year, in which the Liberal Government was returned.

In the North-West Territories the elections were contested upon the question of education. A government, under the leadership of the Hon. Frederick Haultain, was elected, pledged to unify the **school system,** and bring both Separate and Public schools under the same regulations as to text-books, the qualifications of teachers, and the inspection of schools. The bill, which the Assembly passed for this purpose, added another grievance to the number already protested against throughout the Dominion, by the supporters of the absolute distinction of Separate from Public schools.

Manitoba and the North-West Territories received a large influx of immigrants, many coming in from the United States. The result has been, that these portions of the Dominion have fulfilled their promise of being the best wheat-lands of the Continent.

7. In Ontario, the Hon. George A. Kirkpatrick was appointed to the lieutenant-governorship. In August, the Legislature celebrated the **100th anniversary** of its existence, by assembling at Niagara (Old Newark), where the first meeting of the Legislature of Upper Canada was held in 1792.*

8. In Quebec, the election which followed the dismissal of the Mercier Ministry took place on the 8th of March, and a House of Assembly was returned, which contained only fourteen of Mr. Mercier's supporters. There was a good deal of discussion over the **constitutional question,** which grew out of the action of

---

*See page 52.

Lieutenant-Governor Angers. The last meeting of the Assembly having ended on the 30th of December, 1890, and the election intervening, there was no session for twelve months, as there should have been under the terms of the Confederation Act. Public opinion, however, sustained the Lieutenant-Governor in the peculiar crisis, which gave rise to the dismissal of the former ministry. The new government, in order to retrieve the credit of the Province in regard to its public debt, put in force a strict economy, and likewise had to resort to a measure of direct taxation. The Hon. J. A. Chapleau was made Lieutenant-Governor, in the place of the Hon. Mr. Angers, who took a seat in the Dominion Cabinet.

In May, **Montreal** celebrated the 250th anniversary of her founding as Marianapolis.

9. In New Brunswick, by an Act passed in 1891, the **Legislative Council** was abolished, and in 1892, the provincial elections returned a House of Assembly, which continued the Ministry of the Hon. A. Blair in power.

For some time, the **mineral resources** of Nova Scotia had received a great deal of attention, as to their extent and value, which, in 1892, showed a beneficial result in their development. English capitalists were led to invest largely in the opening up of old and new mines, and there was a large increase in the output of the several minerals. The minerals, which are found in large quantities and of the best quality, are gold, iron, gypsum, antimony, copper and coal. Of the latter, the New England States take a large quantity, in spite of the heavy United States duties.

The total output of the mining industries of the Dominion for the year was $19,000,000.

10. Owing to continued ill health, Sir John Abbott resigned the premiership in November, and was succeeded by **Sir John Thompson**, the Minister of Justice.

11. The Dominion Parliament of 1893 met on the 26th of January, and was prorogued on the 1st of April. The session was short and full of incident. The "tariff question" received the largest share of attention. The exclusiveness of the United States duties had caused a good deal of expression of opinion in Canada,

and it was suggested that our duties should be altered to favor Great Britain, which had always afforded Canada an open market. Mr. Dalton McCarthy, who had hitherto ranked as a firm protectionist, introduced a motion to the effect that the Canadian duties, having served their purpose in fostering manufacturing industries, should now be lowered and re-arranged, so as to **favor trade** with **Great Britain** and other parts of the Empire. Foreign countries, and especially the United States, were to have the benefits of the changes in like manner, whenever they reciprocated in favor of our exports to them. This motion was, however, negatived by a vote of 116 to 61.

The debate brought from the Government the announcement, that the Minister of Finance, the Hon. Mr. Foster, the Minister of Trade and Commerce, the Hon. Mr. Bowell, and the Controllers of Customs and Inland Revenue, the Hon. Messrs. Wallace and Jones, would, during the remainder of the year, hold personal interviews, in the several sections of the Dominion, with representative merchants, farmers and manufacturers. This procedure was for the purpose of testing the tariff, by the experience of those who operated under it, and so learn in what way it would be to the country's interest to alter it.

12. While this debate was in progress, Sir Charles Tupper, the High Commissioner, was seeking to make a **treaty** with **France** —a country which has a **double tariff**, similar to that advocated by Mr. McCarthy, namely, a maximum and minimum rate of duties, the latter for those countries which favor France in the exchange of products. This new treaty proposed, that we should give France the benefit of any reductions made by us in any future treaties with other countries. A clause of this kind in treaties is called **the most favored nation clause**, and has its merits if it operates both ways. But the new treaty, while stipulating that Canada should so favor France, did not bind France to similar action in favor of Canada. When, therefore, the treaty came before our Parliament to be ratified, its one-sidedness caused disappointment, and its ratification was laid over till the following session. This postponement threatened to make it very embarrassing for the Ministry.

The Finance Minister stated, that the High Commissioner had been instructed regarding the objections to "the most favored nation clause," as proposed in the **French Treaty**, but Sir Charles Tupper affirmed on the other hand, that the despatch giving the objections did not reach him, until after the time had passed when the treaty was to be signed. He therefore asked, that the Ministry should take the **responsibility** of his action and ratify the treaty. The postponement, therefore, by the Ministry of such action, raised the hopes of the Opposition, that the Ministry had placed itself in the difficult position of being obliged to ratify the treaty, or accept the resignation of Sir Charles Tupper as High Commissioner.

13. **A point of procedure** was also the subject of debate. The Legislature of Nova Scotia had passed an Act, by which a company with United States capital had become owners of large coal mining interests in Cape Breton. The local opposition to the company, having failed to prevent its charter being granted, sent a delegation to ask the Governor-General to disallow the Act of the Legislature. He referred them to his Ministers. The question arose, as to the right of petitioning the Governor-General in person, instead of through his Ministers. It was claimed, during the debate, that all subjects have the right to approach Her Majesty, or Her Majesty's representative, by **petition**, whether verbal or written. The question of veto in this instance was decided by Sir John Thompson's affirming, that the mines belonged to the Province of Nova Scotia, and therefore the Federal Government would not interfere.

CHAPTER XXIII.

BEHRING SEA SEALING QUESTION.

1. Points of dispute.
2. Court of Arbitration.
3. Questions and Decisions.
4. Regulations—Honors.
5. Liberal Convention at Ottawa.
6. World's Fair.
7. The Earl of Aberdeen Governor-General.
8. Death of Sir A. T. Galt and Sir J. J. C. Abbott.
9. The Hon. Mackenzie Bowell's mission to Australia.
10. Temperance Plebiscite.
11. Separate School Question.
12. Treaty with France.
13. The Colonies and the Empire.

1. 1893.—Parliament was no sooner prorogued, than the attention of the country was turned to Paris.

The **Behring Sea Sealing Question** had, during the past three years, been the subject of much correspondence between the governments of the United States and Great Britain. The United States claimed **two things** in regard to this question. First, that the Behring Sea was a "closed sea," its southern limits being the Aleutian Islands, and, therefore, the sealing vessels of other nations had no right there. Secondly, that the home of the seals was upon the Pribyloff Islands, belonging to the United States, and, therefore, although the animals went beyond the three-mile limit for feeding purposes, they were still United States property, and sealers of other nations had no right to hunt them. Upon the presumption of these claims, Canadian sealers had been prevented pursuing their calling, and several vessels had been seized by United States cruisers.

2. The two governments had at last agreed to submit the whole dispute of "national rights" to a **Court of Arbitration**, made up of representatives chosen by the governments of France, Italy, and Norway and Sweden, along with two each to be appointed by Great Britain and the United States. The members of the Court were all men eminent for their judicial training, and knowledge of international law. Great Britain selected as its members of the Court, Lord Chief Justice Hannen and Sir John Thompson, Premier of our Dominion.

Eminent counsel on each side did the pleading of his country. For Great Britain there were Sir Richard Webster and Sir Charles

Russell, and for Canada, Christopher Robinson, Q.C., while the Hon. C. H. Tupper, our Minister of Marine, was in attendance at the Court as agent, to watch the interests of Great Britain and Canada.

3. It was further agreed by Great Britain and the United States, that the dispute as to "national rights" should be submitted to the Court in the form of five questions, and a decision asked upon each. The **questions** and their respective **decisions** were as follows:

(1) What exclusive jurisdiction in the Behring Sea, and what exclusive rights in the seal fisheries, had Russia prior and up to the time of the cession of Alaska to the United States?

Decision.—Russia never asserted, in fact, or exercised any exclusive jurisdiction in Behring Sea, or any exclusive rights in the seal fisheries therein, beyond the ordinary limit of territorial waters.

(2) How far were these claims of jurisdiction conceded by Great Britain?

Decision.—Great Britain did not recognize or concede any claim upon the part of Russia to exclusive jurisdiction as to the seal fisheries in Behring Sea, outside of territorial waters.

(3) Was the body of water, now known as the Behring Sea, included in the phrase "Pacific Ocean," as used in the treaty of 1825 between Great Britain and Russia, and what rights, if any, in the Behring Sea were held and exclusively exercised by Russia after said treaty?

Decision.—The body of water, now known as Behring Sea, was included in the phrase "Pacific Ocean," as used in said treaty. No exclusive rights of jurisdiction in Behring Sea, and no exclusive rights as to the seal fisheries therein were held or exercised by Russia, outside of ordinary territorial waters after said treaty of 18_5.

(4) Did not all the rights of Russia in the treaty between the United States and Russia, of March 30th, 1867, pass unimpaired to the United States under that treaty?

Decision.—That all the rights of Russia as to jurisdiction and as to the seal fisheries in Behring Sea, east of the water boundary, in the treaty between the United States and Russia, of 1867, did pass unimpaired to the United States under the said treaty.

(5) Has the United States any right of protection or property in the fur-seals frequenting the islands of the United States in Behring Sea, when such seals are found outside the ordinary three-mile limit ?

Decision.—The United States has not any right of jurisdiction or property in the fur-seals frequenting the islands of the United States in Behring Sea, when such seals are found outside the ordinary three-mile limit.

4. These decisions were given on the 15th of August, after which certain **regulations** were laid down as to the *season* in which seals were to be hunted, the use of *instruments* in killing them, and the *licensing* of vessels engaged in the trade. It was also forbidden that any seals should be taken within a zone of sixty miles of the Pribyloff Islands, owned by the United States. The result of the arbitration was in its decisions a **justification** of Canadian sealers in the past, while in the regulations, a wholesome **restraint** was sought to be placed upon the former freedom of vessels of all nations engaging in the hunt. This was thought necessary for the protection of seal life, by preventing their ruthless destruction. As a recognition of their services upon the arbitration, Sir John Thompson was made a Privy Councillor of Great Britain, and the Hon. C. H. Tupper received the honor of knighthood. The same honor was conferred upon Christopher Robinson, Q.C., which he however asked permission to decline.

5. Meanwhile, in Canada, the public attention was not wholly absorbed in what was being done at Paris.

In June there was gathered at Ottawa, a notable convention of the **Liberal Party** of the Dominion, the delegates to which numbered nearly two thousand. The object of the convention was to review the past action of the party upon "public questions," and to assert the position it should take upon such questions in the future. Sir Oliver Mowat presided. The convention pledged itself as follows : That the **Tariff** should be freer than at present, so as to promote more general trade, especially with Great Britain and the United States ; and that a **Reciprocity Treaty** should be sought with the latter country. That the **Franchise Act** for the Dominion elections should be based upon the same qualifications, as for the election of members for the legislatures in the several provinces. That the **Redistribution Act** should be amended, so that the boundaries of counties should mark the constituencies for the Dominion Parliament. That the **Senate** should be elective ; and that the sentiment of the people in reference to **Prohibition** should be learned by means of a **plebiscite** vote of the Dominion.

6. The **World's Fair** was opened at Chicago on the 1st of May, this year, and continued until the 1st of October. For two years the preparations had been in progress, and no expense had been spared to make the Fair the largest, the most beautiful in effect, and the most representative of all that had ever been held. It was made, also, a celebration of the four hundredth anniversary of the landing of Columbus in America, and thereby received the name of the "Columbian Exposition." The buildings and their surroundings covered nearly a thousand acres. Canada's exhibits occupied a space of seventy thousand square feet, representing in detail the products of her fields, mines, forests, and manufactures. The Dominion Commissioners in charge of her interests were Mr. G. R. R. Cockburn, M.P., the Hon. Joseph Tassé and Mr. J. S. Larke. The Provincial Commissioners were Mr. C. J. Law, for British Columbia ; Senator Perley, for the North-West ; Mr. Awrey, M.P.P., for Ontario, and the Hon. Mr. McIntosh, for Quebec. The awards given to Canada upon her various exhibits numbered about two thousand. In the Department of Education, she stood first in all the matters of school appliances, and text-books, and methods of teaching and administration.

7. In July, the Governor-General, who had come to us as Lord Stanley, took his departure from Canada. During his term of office he had succeeded to the title of Earl of Derby, upon the death of his brother. Lord Derby has continued to evince a warm friendship for the Dominion. General Montgomery was sworn in as Administrator until the **Earl of Aberdeen** should arrive, in September, to take up the duties laid down by Lord Derby.

8. Like its predecessor, 1893 bears the record of the death of two men who had been eminent in the service of Canada. **Sir Alex. T. Galt**, another of the fathers of Confederation and late High Commissioner to Great Britain, died on the 22nd of September.

Sir J. J. C. Abbott, within a year of his resignation of the premiership of the Dominion, passed from this life on the 31st of October.

9. To no nation, have the improvements in the use of electricity and steam been of so marked a benefit, as to the British Empire. Her colonies and dependencies, scattered far and near over the surface of the globe, have been brought within speaking distance by the telegraph, while fast railway and steamship service has reduced the distance from months to weeks, and from weeks to days. Following the establishment of the Canadian steamship line between our western coast and Japan and China, we have now a **direct line** between the same western ports and Australia. Although recent, so important has become the influence of this connection, that the Government gave the Hon. Mr. Bowell, Minister of Trade and Commerce, a mission to **Australia** and **New Zealand**, to promote our further intercourse and trade with these British colonies on the other side of the world. Mr. Bowell left for Australia in the fall, and returned in January, 1894. He was most hospitably entertained, while the subject of his mission was discussed in a business-like manner. The colonies in the South Sea laid large stress upon **two things**—cable connection with Canada, and a more frequent steamship service. It was arranged that, in the coming summer, a **conference** should be held at Ottawa, to which all the colonies should be invited to send delegates.

10. 1894.—For several years the Dominion Alliance has been desirous of ascertaining the sentiment of the provinces in regard to **Prohibition**, by means of what is called a *plebiscite* vote, that is, a vote of opinion. Such a vote had already been taken in Prince Edward Island, Nova Scotia and Manitoba, showing a majority in these provinces in favor of such a measure. In 1893, the Legislature of Ontario, in answer to petitions, arranged that a plebiscite should be taken in that province in January, 1894, in connection with the municipal elections. The vote gave a majority of over 80,000 in favor of Prohibition. The Alliance at once asked the Government to bring forward a bill to forbid the manufacture, as well as the sale, of intoxicating liquors within the Province. A new phase of this question then appeared, namely, whether the Province had

the right, under the British North America Act, to pass such a measure. This question is now before the Supreme Court of Canada for its opinion.

11. Early in the year the same court gave its opinion upon the **Separate School** question, referred to it by the Dominion Government. When the Privy Council in England gave the decision, which, in effect, confirmed the Manitoba School Act of 1890 as constitutional, the Roman Catholic minority of that province made an appeal to the Governor-General-in-Council, that a remedial Act should be passed by the Dominion Parliament for their benefit. This right of appeal was claimed to be in accordance with a clause of the British North America Act, regarding provinces which had a Separate School system at the time of the Union. The question arose here, whether this appeal was allowable under that Act, and the opinion of the Supreme Court of Canada was asked, upon a series of questions covering the ground of the appeal. The Court decided that the British North America Act did not give the right to the remedial legislation asked for in the appeal.

From the North-West Territories, also, came large petitions to the Dominion Cabinet for disallowance of the School Ordinance, passed in 1892 by the Assembly of the Territories. It was decided, however, not to disallow the Ordinance, but the Executive Council of the North-West was recommended, so to modify the operation of the Ordinance, as to meet the desires of the supporters of their Separate Schools.

12. Regarding the questions of **trade** and **tariffs**, the Dominion Parliament voted the ratification of the Treaty with France. The vote was somewhat independent of party lines. The people of Quebec held a large sentiment in favor of the treaty; the Government supporters felt that the public honor was committed to its being ratified, and whatever objection there had been, on account of "the most favored nation clause," was weakened by a clause of the treaty, which permitted it to be ended upon a year's notice.

Following the interviews held throughout the country the preceding year by members of the Government, regarding the operation of the tariff, the Finance Minister introduced a bill making many changes in the duties upon various articles of commerce. The *protective* character of the tariff was, however, maintained.

13. The leading event of the year has been the meeting at Ottawa of the **Inter-Colonial Conference**, arranged for by the Hon. Mackenzie Bowell during his visit to Australia. On the 28th of June, the first session was opened in the Senate Chamber, with addresses of welcome by His Excellency, Lord Aberdeen, and the Right Hon. Sir John Thompson, and responses by the delegates of the other colonies, and by the Earl of Jersey, the delegate from the Home Government. Besides the Imperial delegate, there were representatives from the Colonies of Tasmania, New South Wales, South Australia, New Zealand, Victoria, Queensland, and Cape Colony. The Canadian delegates were the Hon. Mackenzie Bowell, the Hon. Sir Adolphe Caron and Sandford Fleming, C.M.G.

The Hon. Mackenzie Bowell was elected President of the Conference. Its sessions closed on the 11th of July. Resolutions were passed, urging the improvement of the steamship service to Australia, and the importance of a British cable connection with the South Sea Colonies, by way of the Pacific Ocean and Canada. The resolution, however, which more largely attracted the public sympathy, was one advocating, between Great Britain and her Colonies, a customs arrangement which would favor their mutual trade. In a word, the Conference declared itself in favor of a *preferential tariff* for the Empire. If such shall not be found practicable at once, this resolution is, at least, the expression, by the most influential British Colonies, of a desire for the federation of the Empire.

Looking back over Canada's history, we see the five well-marked paths of **national policy,** along which her statesmen of all parties have walked and worked. These are:

1. A jealous attention to the subjects and methods of public education.

2. A high regard for public honor.

3. The strengthening of internal relations by loyal appeal to her constitution.

4. The proper assertion of her rights in international relations.

5. A national ambition to fill worthily the important place Canada holds in the circle of the Empire.

CHAPTER XXIV.

CONSTITUTION AND GOVERNMENT.

1. The English Constitution.
2. The Great Charter.
3. Primary Principles.
4. The Dominion Act.
5. Limited Monarchy in Canada.
6. Duties of the Governor-General.
7. The Senate.
8. The Election to the Commons.
9. The House of Commons—Procedure.
10. Selection of the Cabinet.
11. Privy Council in Canada.
12. The influence of public sentiment.

1. We have seen that previous to the union of 1867, each province of the Dominion had its system of government, similar to that of the Mother Country, and which it had acquired after a greater or less struggle by petition and agitation. Throughout the several stages of colonial growth, as marked by these efforts after self-government, and by the Imperial Acts granted in response to them, there was a constant appeal made to that authority called the **English Constitution**, in the provisions of which, the people of the provinces claimed to have equal rights, with their fellow-subjects in Great Britain. And not only by means of petition, but also throughout the whole course of legislation, we find reference made to the same standard. If we pass from Canadian to English history, and follow it back for more than six hundred years, we shall find this same authority appealed to again and again, not merely as a guide in peaceful law-making, but as the only basis for the settlement of national struggles far more protracted and fierce, than any that have ever occurred in the colonies. From these facts it would seem, that at some time in the past, there had been an agreement between the several classes of the population in the kingdom, concerning their mutual duties, rights, and privileges in their government.

2. And such was the case, for as far back as 1215, when King John had so abused his power, that all classes of the people could endure it no longer, we find that the lords, bishops, and commons of England met the king in a large plain on the banks of the Thames, near London, in order to consider the state of the kingdom. He was reminded that he received his sovereignty by the assent of his subjects and that he had violated his oath, taken

when crowned, to govern according to the laws. He was given the choice of doing the right or of having his sovereignty given to another. The result was a parchment of mutual agreement, signed by the King on the one hand, and by the leading subjects on the other. This parchment, which has ever since been called the **Great Charter**, has been subscribed to by successive Sovereigns. It has been followed by other similar covenants, and by legislation, which has had the effect of developing and confirming its great **primary principles**, and extending their application. These principles are said to form the basis of the English Constitution, and may be briefly stated as follows:

*3. (1) "The government of the country by an hereditary "sovereign, ruling with limited powers, and bound to summon and "consult a parliament of the whole realm, comprising peers, and "elective representatives of the commons.

(2) "That without the sanction of Parliament, no tax of any "kind can be imposed, and no law can be made, repealed or "altered.

(3) "That no man be arbitrarily fined or imprisoned, that no "man's property or liberties be impaired, and that no man be in "any way punished, except after a lawful trial.

(4) "Trial by jury.

(5) "That justice shall not be sold or delayed."

From the above facts and statements we learn: (1) that the English nation has always preferred an hereditary sovereign as its executive head; (2) that the authority of the monarch has been conferred by the people, and (3) that, as confirmed by history, these two facts have been assented to by sovereigns and parliaments for centuries, and that when a sovereign has violated his oath, the nation has transferred that authority to another, but always of the same family.

The sovereign power of a nation is two-fold. It is a **legislative** power, and makes laws for the welfare of the people. It is also **executive** in its nature and can enforce obedience to law. The power which the English people confer upon their Sovereign is shared by them, for purposes of legislation. The parliament

---

* Creasy on the English Constitution.

consists of the Sovereign, Lords, and Commons, called the three estates of the realm. A committee of the Commons advises the Sovereign as to the exercise of his power in enforcing the laws. (See page 72.)

4. This system of government, which is called a **limited Monarchy**, has been transferred by Great Britain to her colonies, by means of the Special Acts* of Parliament passed for that purpose.

The last of such Special Acts was that of 1867, the "British North America Act," which, out of the several separate colonies, with as many constitutions, all nearly alike, created the "Dominion of Canada," and gave it a constitution of its own. The union then formed has been called a *federacy*, or *confederation*, because the terms of a constitution which joins provinces or states together for certain purposes, and leaves them independent for others, are esteemed to have all the force of the terms of a *treaty*.

Having already mentioned the leading provisions of our present system of government, and the incidents of their operation, it will be useful to note in them the application of the principles, which marked our former constitutions, as well as that of England.

5. The Act of 1867 affirms the principle of the limited Monarchy, the executive power of and over Canada being vested in the Queen. The Parliament of Canada consists of the Queen, the Senate, and the Commons. The Queen acts through her representative, the Governor-General, who, upon his arrival in the Dominion, takes an oath to exercise the Sovereign authority reposed in him, according to the laws of the Dominion, and **with the advice** of the Queen's Privy Council-in-Canada, or rather that portion of it which at the time may have the support of the House of Commons.

6. The duties of the Governor-General to be thus exercised, are briefly as follows :

(1) The appointment of Lieutenant-Governors in the Provinces, and their removal within five years, upon sufficient cause.

(2) The appointment of Judges to the various courts, and their removal upon the address of Parliament.

(3) The commuting of the sentence of a court of justice.

---

* See pages 46, 48, 72, 77, and 93.

(4) The members of the Senate being appointed by the Crown, the Governor-General must summon persons duly qualified, to fill any vacancies that may occur in that body. He also appoints one of their number as Speaker of the Senate, and may remove him.

(5) He calls together the House of Commons, and may dissolve it within the five years for which it had been elected.

(6) Although by the constitution, the Sovereign is one of the elements of Parliament, the Governor-General, like the Sovereign in England, takes no part in legislation, but in the Sovereign's name assents to bills which have passed both Houses. He may, however, refuse such assent, or reserve the bills in question for the Royal consideration.

(7) He may disallow Acts of a Provincial Legislature within one year after their having been passed in the Province.

7. As pointed out in the English Constitution, the realm is said to consist of three estates, the Sovereign, Lords, and Commons. In Canada there are but two, the Sovereign, and the Commons. A place, however, has been made in our Constitution for an Upper House, called the **Senate**, which, on account of the position it thus holds, resembles somewhat that of the House of Lords in England. The Senate was thought necessary, in order to prevent hasty legislation, and to preserve, as it were, the balance of the Constitution. Senators must hold property to the value of $4,000 above all debts, and have passed the age of thirty years. They are selected on account of their standing in the country, experience in Parliament or other public affairs. The number of Senators created in 1867 was seventy-two, and though since increased by the admission of other provinces, that number can never exceed eighty-two, which may be reached if Newfoundland shall enter the Confederation. In session, fifteen members including the Speaker form a quorum. All questions are decided by a majority of votes, the Speaker casting his vote, in every instance, with the others. If the number of votes for and against a measure are equal, the measure is said to be lost. With regard to **legislation**, money-bills are the only ones excepted from commencing in the Senate, and it is necessary that all bills should pass the Senate **before receiving** the assent of the Governor-General. Legislation upon any measure is stopped if the vote of the Senate is against

10

the measure, although it may have passed the Commons. In this respect, the Senate of Canada has more power than the House of Lords, for if the latter "throws out" a bill of the English Commons, the Commons may recommend the Crown to create as many new lords, as shall be sufficient to carry the measure in the Upper House. The Canadian Commons cannot do this, the number of the Senators being limited by the Act of 1867.

8. Besides what has already been said regarding the **House of Commons**, it may be added that the provinces are divided into electoral districts or ridings, for the purpose of representation in this House. Each district or riding declares by a majority of votes its selection of a member. If a vacancy occurs in the representation of a riding, a new writ, or summons must be issued to the riding to elect another member. All writs of election are issued by the Clerk of the Crown in Chancery, and are directed to the Sheriff or Registrar of the district, or other person appointed for the purpose, who conducts the election, and who must make a return of the votes cast or polled if more than one candidate is "running" for election. If there is only one he is declared elected by acclamation. Candidates must be subjects of the Crown, are not required to have a property qualification, and must not hold any office or place of profit under the Crown, or contract in the gift of the Government.

9. Each parliament is elected for five years, and holds its sessions every year during that time, unless dissolved. The House elects its own Speaker. Twenty members, including the Speaker, constitute a quorum. All questions coming before the House are decided by a majority of the votes of its members, the Speaker voting only when the vote of the House is a "tie." All bills may originate here; money-bills must do so. The great power of the House of Commons lies in the fact that it possesses the control of the revenue of the country, and may upon occasion refuse the **Supply Bill**, which is necessary for the expenses of government.

10. Every subject of the state is supposed to be represented in the House of Commons, for the purpose of exercising that important element of the constitution—the limiting power. There are always **public questions** before the country, upon which there is a greater or less variety and strength of opinion. As these questions

form the *issues* upon which elections are held, the result of the elections gives the public sentiment of the majority of the electors in the country, and therefore what will be the prevailing sentiment in the **Commons**. It is this sentiment which it is important that the Crown, that is, the Governor-General, should know. Having summoned parliament, he calls upon that member of the Commons who possesses the confidence of its majority, to select others, members either of the Commons or the Senate, who with him shall become advisers of the Crown, in conducting the business of the country. If the member of Commons thus honored accepts the task, and is successful in persuading others to share the responsibility with him, he becomes the **Leader** of the Government, and is called the **Prime Minister**, or First Minister. His associates in the Government are styled Ministers of the Crown, or of State, Members of the Cabinet, or of the Government, and Privy Councillors. Upon assuming office they must take a special oath as to their new duties. Those who are members of the Commons, must present themselves as early as possible before their ridings for re-election, as a test of the public feeling regarding their acceptance of office. The **Dominion Cabinet** consists of thirteen members, one of whom becomes President of the Privy Council, each of the remaining twelve becoming the head of some one of the departments, into which the work of carrying on the Government is divided, namely, the Departments of Justice, Finance, Agriculture, Secretary of State of Canada, Militia and Defence, Trade and Commerce (includes Customs), Inland Revenue, the Interior, Public Works, Railways and Canals, Marine and Fisheries, and the Post Office Department.

11. The Ministry hold office so long as they continue to hold the confidence of the majority in the Commons. When that fails them they are obliged to resign, and the Crown repeats its former steps in order to supply their place. The members of a late Ministry, however, remain during life, under the obligation of their special oath, and should the majority in the Commons again support them, may again be called on in the same way as before, to assume the *active* duties of government. Out of office they continue to be Privy Councillors. The term **Privy Council-in-Canada**, then, includes all those who are now, or have been,

under the late Act, advisers of the Crown; while the terms Cabinet, Ministry, and Administration should be **applied only** to those Privy Councillors, who at any time actually fill the Departments of the State.

12. Following the sentiment which supports it in the Commons, every Cabinet has a **policy** or method, according to which it proposes to conduct the Government to the greatest advantage of the state, and upon this policy it bases its claim to continued support. If its policy is not supported, the Ministry is said to be defeated, and resigns. Its members, however, generally become the leaders of the **minority** in the House, and watch carefully the *policy* of their successors, seeking, if possible, to turn public sentiment again in favor of their own. The *adherents* of a public policy acting together form a *political party*, while the statement, attack, and defence of a policy constitute the business of *politics*. The Crown takes no part in the strife of policy, but is an interested spectator, and discovers by means of it the policy which has the support of the country. The leader in the Commons of the party holding this policy, is that member upon whom the Crown **must call** to select its responsible advisers. He is thus the double choice of the country and the Crown. * "And our Constitution "does not admit of the supposition that the Crown will choose "anyone not the choice of the people. The Cabinet, in effect, "governs the people; and the people only have to say of whom "the Cabinet is to be composed. It is their loss or gain, and is "their choice by right. The Crown approves without interfering."

---

* See " Manual of Government in Canada," by D. A. O'Sullivan, M.A.

CHAPTER XXV.

CONSTITUTION AND GOVERNMENT—(*Continued*).

1. The Provinces before and after 1867.
2. Present Legislatures.
3. Provincial Ministry.
4. Duties of Ministry in Ontario.
5. Municipal Government.
6. Educational Government.
7. Executive power of the Constitution.
8. Distributed to administer the law.
9. Courts of Justice.
10. The Chief Magistrate.

1. By the Act of 1867, the Imperial Parliament only confirmed the free action of the **Provinces**, whose relationship thus became changed. Until then, with the exception of the two Canadas, they were independent of one another, but each stood in a like position of direct relations with the Home Government. Their governors were the direct representatives of the Crown. Their legislatures also considered every matter pertaining to their respective provinces in all their relations. Having become parts of the **Dominion**, there is now but one direct representative of the Crown for them all—the Governor-General—who appoints their lieutenant-governors and may remove them. Having given up to the Dominion Parliament extensive powers of legislation with reference to their mutual relations, their own powers of legislation are now limited to certain **specified subjects** relating to their internal management. Beyond these subjects they may not go, but upon them the Dominion Parliament may not trespass.

2. By the Act of 1867, all laws formerly in force in the provinces were continued, and each province retained the form of its legislature, and method of procedure therein, along with the power to modify these as occasion might require. Accordingly we find the form of legislature existing in some provinces to consist of one House, and in others of two Houses. In Prince Edward Island the members of the second House or Legislative Council are elected, while in Nova Scotia, New Brunswick and Quebec they are appointed by the Lieutenant-Governors. The numbers of members of the Provincial Legislatures are as follows :

	Legislative Assembly.	Legislative Council.
Prince Edward Island	33	13
Nova Scotia	37	17
New Brunswick	41	17
Quebec	65	24
Ontario	88	
Manitoba	20	
British Columbia	25	

In 1891 and '92 the Legislative Councils of New Brunswick and Prince Edward Island were abolished by Acts of their own Parliaments.

3. The units of the Legislature in each province are the Lieutenant-Governor, and either one or two Houses, as just mentioned, with an **Executive Council**, which is the Ministry of the Province, with duties and methods of procedure, similar to those of the Dominion Cabinet. It must have a *policy* of its own, and possess the confidence of the Legislative Assembly. Its members are the heads of Departments in the work of provincial government.

4. In **Ontario** the Ministry is composed of six members, among whom the work of administration is at present divided as follows, the duties of each department being somewhat suggested by the title:

(1) The Attorney-General for the Province, who is responsible for the character of the legislative work of the Assembly. His duties resemble largely those of the Minister of Justice in the Dominion Cabinet.

(2) The Provincial Secretary.

(3) The Provincial Treasurer.

(4) The Commissioner of Crown Lands.

(5) The Commissioner of Agriculture and Public Works.

(6) The Minister of Education.

In the other provinces the Department of Education is under the supervision of officers styled Superintendents of Education.

5. By legislation under both their former and present constitutions, all the provinces have provided for the government of counties, townships, cities, towns, and villages, by themselves, in many matters relating only to the inhabitants within their limits. These local governments, called **Municipalities**, or Municipal Corporations, are regulated in the extent of their powers by

statutes of their provincial legislatures, called Munic.pal Acts. Two or more municipalities may be united to form a joint corporation. The form of government is a local council, elected yearly by the votes of the inhabitants. In cities those elected are styled aldermen; in all others, councillors. The executive heads of the municipalities have various titles, being called Mayors, in cities and towns, and Reeves in townships and villages. Both Mayors and Reeves are elected directly by the voters. In the case of counties, the council in each is made up of the reeves and deputy-reeves of the townships and villages, and sometimes towns, within the county limits. The county council, at its first meeting, elects one of its number as its Warden or chief officer.

All these corporations have a limited power of legislation, and measures passed by them are called By-laws.

6. For the promotion of the **Education** of the youth of Canada, there has grown up a *three-fold system* of schools. These are, first, **Primary Schools**, which include both Public and Separate Schools; secondly, **High Schools**, which stand midway between the Primary Schools and Universities; and thirdly, the **Universities**. These all exist under *law*.

For the support and **government** of **Primary Schools**, all the municipalities of the provinces are divided into **school sections**, with the exception of cities, towns, and villages, each of which is a section in itself. These sections form corporations in themselves, quite distinct from all others, and composed of three or more members called Trustees. They receive their powers and are guided in their use of them, by provincial statutes, called School Acts. They must also carry out the special instructions issued by the Minister of Education for the Province. They have authority as to the expenses of education within their limits, and in order to meet such expenses must either directly, or through their municipal corporation, levy and collect the necessary amount from the ratepayers. Their enactments are called Resolutions. The school sections of each municipality, or of a collection of municipalities, form a district for the purposes of government inspection, each district being under an officer called an Inspector of Schools, and who, being properly qualified, is appointed by the chief municipal council of the district. The

Inspector is guided in his duties by the regulations of the Department of Education.

Again, upon application to the Department of Education, a municipality, or collection of municipalities, may be constituted a **District,** for the maintenance of one or more **High Schools** within its limits. As to **government**, each such school has its own Corporate Board of Trustees, whose duties are defined by statutes, called High School Acts. These schools come directly under the supervision of the Department of Education, which appoints the officers for their inspection (without reference to the municipalities), and issues regulations 'as to their equipment and course of study.

The **Universities**, which form the third class of schools, have been founded by the munificence of individuals, religious denominations, or provincial governments. Each university forms a corporate body, constituted either under a charter, or special statute, which defines the powers of the corporation, and gives it authority to **teach,** and confer **degrees,** in one or more of the **faculties** of learning.

7. In the foregoing outline of the construction of government, necessary to law-making or legislation under our Constitution, we see that the people of Canada are solely responsible for the laws, by which their individual and public duties are regulated, from the enactment of the School Board to the Acts of the Dominion Parliament. All laws carry with them certain *penalties* or *forfeitures,* to be inflicted in cases where the laws are violated, and which are presumed to equal the offence against the law in question. Every enactment, moreover, whether by-law or statute, being for the public welfare, carries with it the **authority** for its *enforcement,* and for this purpose calls for the exercise of the **Executive power** in the Constitution. As we have seen, the executive power is part of the power bestowed upon the **Sovereign,** to be held and exercised as advised by the people themselves, through the Cabinet or Ministry.

8. In order that this executive power may be exercised promptly, and in every part of the realm, it has been distributed to all Governors in their provinces, Ministers in their departments, Wardens, Mayors, Reeves, and many others, specially appointed, and called

Justices of the Peace. All these have power, according to the statutes guiding them, to **administer** the laws, that is, to proclaim them and see that they are obeyed, or the penalty enforced. In this capacity these officers are called **Magistrates**.

9. But there have always been many occasions in the administration of the laws, when there was less or more doubt as to their meaning and application, respecting the "rights, duties, and privileges" of the people. In early times when the nation was only a tribe, the head of the tribe, as **Chief Magistrate**, administered the laws. In doing so he not only made them known, but enforced their observance, and explained them in instances of doubt. In all cases of trial he was the sole **judge** between the people, and exercised this power before the fellow-subjects of the accused. And such was the practice after the tribe became a nation, the king authorizing **others to assist** him in these duties. In the Great Charter we see that the people stipulated for a "lawful trial," and a "trial by jury," that is, before a sworn number of their fellow-subjects. This early practice and these stipulations were the beginnings of that wide system of **Courts of Justice**, which are presided over by judges "learned in the laws," and which, throughout the year, and through all the land, decide as to the law between man and man, and even between provinces and parliaments. These judges derive their authority from the same source as the magistrates, and in the courts are themselves bound by special statutes, as to how they shall explain the laws and decide by them.

10. There are many courts in the realm, but to-day the **highest** is that of the Queen, advised by her Privy Council. The Sovereign is still the Chief Magistrate. The Sovereign power is not given away, it is only shared with the people for their benefit, and remains in its efficiency where the people conferred it in the Constitution, for the two-fold purpose of making and enforcing the laws.

PRONUNCIATION OF FRENCH NAMES.

In the right-hand column all the vowels, whether long or short, have their ordinary English sound, except in the case of *en, an, on* and *in*. These are called nasal sounds in French. The force of *an, en* and *on* is very nearly that of *on* in the English word *wrong*, while the sound of *in* resembles that of *en* in the English word *strength*. These nasal sounds will be indicated by *italics*. J in French has the sound of z in *azure*, and may be represented by *zh*. The syllables of French words must receive an **equal stress** of the voice in pronunciation. As this causes French words to sound to an *English ear*, as if they were accented upon the last syllable, an accent mark has been placed over the *last syllable* in the right hand column, to remind English pupils to give special stress to that syllable. By doing so, and pronouncing the other syllables lightly, they will acquire more nearly the French sound. Notice that *Cabot* is not a French word,

Aix-la-Chapelle....Aiks-lä-shäpel'.
Angers...........*An*-zhäy'.
Belleau ....Bel-lō'.
Bigot ....Bee-gō'.
Boucherville ......Boo-shair-veel'.
Cabot ....Cab'-ot.
Caen.............Kä-*en*.
Cataraqui ....Kä-tä-rä-kee'.
Chaleurs ....Shal-lūr'.
Champlain ....Cham-pli*n*'.
Chastes ....Shast.
Chateauguay.....Shä-tō-gay'.
Chauvin ....Shō-vi*n*'.
D'Aillebout ......Day-boo'.
D'Argenson .....Dar-zhen-so*n*'.
D'Avaugour .....Dä-vō-goor'.
De Beauharno's ...Dĕ-bō-har-nwah'.
De Callières .....Dĕ-cäl-yāre'.
De la Barre ......Dĕ-lä-bar'.
Denonville ....Dĕ-non-veel'.
Dieppe....... ....Dee-ĕp'.
Galissonière .....Gä-lis-son-yāre'.
Ghent ....Ghent.
Isle St. Jean .....Eel-si*n*-zhe*n*.
Jacques Cartier ...Zhak Cart-yā'.
Joliette ....Zhŏl-yet'.
Jonquière ....Zhonk-yāre'.
Lacolle ....Lä-cōl'.
Langevin ....Lan-zhŏ-vi*n*'.

Lauson...........Lō-zo*n*'.
Letellier ....Lĕ-tĕl-yā'.
Lévis ....Lev-ce'.
Lepine ....Lŏ-peen'.
Longueuil ....Lo*n*-gay
Maisonneuve .....May-so*n* nŏv'.
Marquette ....Mar-ket.
Masson..........Mäs-so*n*
Maurepas ....More-pä'.
Mercier.........Mŏr-*see*-ā'.
Miquelon........Mee-kel-o*n*'.
Montcalm ....Mon-ko*n*'.
Montmagny .....Mo*n*-man-yee'
Monts ....Mo*n*.
Papineau ....Pä-pee-nō'.
Pierre ....Pee-āre'.
Pontgravé ....Po*n*-grä-vä'.
Quesne ....Kane.
Roberval.........Rŏb-er-val'.
Robitaille ....Rŏb-ee-tāye'.
Rouen ....Roo-*en*.
Rouillé.... ......Roo-ee-yä'.
Royal ....Rwaw-yäl'.
Seignior ....Sŏn-yūr'.
Soissons ....Swaw-so*n*'.
Vaudreuil ......Vō-drä-ee'.
Ventadour ......Ve*n*-ta-door'.
Versailles ....Ver-sāye'.

TOPICAL INDEX.

ACTS AND BILLS—
    Alien Bill 49, 66, 125
    British North America Act..87, 93-95, 104, 108, 112, 142-148
    Canada Temperance Act (Scott Act) 111
    Canada Trade Act.......................................68
    Clergy Reserves Act 83
    Constitutional Act 46-48, 71, 72
    Jesuits' Estates Bill 38, 49, 122, 123
    Manitoba Acts..97
    Militia Act...50, 83
    Municipal Act..78
    Municipal Loan Fund Act 81, 99
    Quebec Act....................................39, 43, 47
    Rebellion Losses' Bill 80
    Rupert's Land Act 96, 114
    School Acts—Common 54, 67, 79, 90, 91, 101, 112, 149
             Manitoba 125, 140
             New Brunswick 150
             North-West Territories 131, 140
    Seigniorial Tenure Act 82
    Union Act, 1840 ....77, 78

ARBITRATIONS—
    Atlantic Fisheries....................................102
    Behring Sea Sealing 135-137
    San Juan 98

BANKS 65, 68, 70, 95

BATTLES—
    Batoche 117
    Chateauguay 61
    Chippewa 62
    Chrysler's Farm 61
    Cut Knife Creek 117
    Detroit 56

156   HISTORY OF CANADA.

BATTLES—(Continued)—
   Fish Creek 117
   Fort Erie 63, 86
   Fort George 58
   Lacolle Mill 62
   Lexington 41
   Louisbourg 37, 90
   Lundy's Lane 63
   Moraviantown 60
   New Orleans 63
   Oswego 62
   Plains of Abraham (Quebec) 37
   Queenston Heights 57
   Ridgeway 86
   Stony Creek 59
   Washington 63
   Windmill 76
   York 58
   Yorktown 41

CANALS 68, 69, 80, 82, 130, 140

CENSUS 25, 26, 33, 40, 47, 71, 85, 95, 106, 130

CITIES—
   Detroit 33, 38, 56
   Fredericton 90, 116
   Halifax 36, 90, 101, 102
   Kingston 30, 53, 58, 60, 62, 76, 78
   London 53, 76
   Montreal 27, 32, 34, 38, 41, 50, 60, 65, 74, 80, 132
   New Westminster 93
   Ottawa 69, 83, 84, 87
   Quebec 24, 26, 32, 33, 37, 38, 41, 48, 49, 79, 80, 81
   Regina 116, 117
   Sault Ste. Marie 30, 130, 140, 95
   St. John, N.B 91, 101, 102
   St. John's, Nfld 84, 89
   Toronto (York) 36, 53, 58, 70, 75, 87
   Vancouver 129
   Victoria 93
   Winnipeg 34, 92, 97, 117

COMPANIES (Trading Monopolies)—
   Hudson Bay 92, 96
   Merchants 22, 25
   North-West 92
   One Hundred Associates 25, 28, 29

TOPICAL INDEX.

CONSTITUTION AND GOVERNMENT 141, 148
    Confederation 74, 85, 87, 93
    Crown Colony 29, 38, 47
    French Rule.....................21, 38, 44, 45, 89, 92
    Legislative Union 74, 77, 84
    Military Rule...................................38, 39, 47
    Municipal Government.............................78, 149
    Provinces (in the Dominion)..........95, 107, 108, 119, 148
    Responsible Government............47, 48, 72, 73, 80, 81,
                              89, 90, 91, 93, 143, 148
    Schools (place in Constitution) 149, 150

CUSTOMS DUTIES (*see* Tariffs)........40, 46, 53, 68, 72, 78, 80, 90,
                        95, 102, 121, 125, 133, 139

DISCOVERERS AND EXPLORERS—
    Cabot..20
    Cartier...20, 21
    Champlain..23-26
    Columbus...19
    Cook..89, 93
    Drake, Frobisher, Gilbert............................22
    Hudson...92
    Joliette and Marquette...............................30
    La Salle..30
    Mackenzie..93

EDUCATION 29, 34, 49, 54, 65, 67, 69, 78, 79, 81, 83, 90, 91,
             95, 100, 101, 107, 112, 125, 131, 140, 149, 150

FENIANS...86, 97, 99

FISHERIES 20, 22, 26, 38, 82, 90, 98, 102, 119, 122, 135

FUR TRADE....................................22, 29, 34, 92

GENERALS (and officers commanding)—
    (The French Governors of Canada were all active Generals.)
    Amherst...............................37, 38, 91, 122
    Barclay...60
    Braddock...36
    Brock 54, 56, 57
    Colborne...74, 76
    Denison...114
    De Salaberry....................................57, 61
    Drummond 61, 62, 63, 64
    Kirke.....................................26, 88, 89
    Macdonell, Col.....................................57

GENERALS, ETC.—(*Continued*)—
  Macdonell, Major..................................58
  McNab...75
  Middleton............................117, 118, 125
  Montcalm..37
  Montgomery......................................41
  Morrison..61
  Murray..................................37, 38, 39
  Otter..117
  Perry...60
  Phipps......................................32, 90
  Prevost.........................54, 58, 63, 64
  Proctor.....................................57, 60
  Riall...................................61, 62, 63
  Sheaffe...57
  Sherbrooke..................................63, 65
  Strange..117
  Tecumseh....................................56, 60
  Vincent.....................................53, 61
  Wolfe...37
  Wolseley...................................97, 114
  Yeo...59

IMMIGRATION 23, 26, 30, 36, 42, 51, 65, 66,
                              80, 90, 91, 118, 129, 131
INDIANS 20, 24, 27, 32, 38, 56, 60, 101, 116, 117

PARLIAMENTS................47, 48, 52, 72, 77, 80, 82, 87, 99,
                              107, 108, 110, 118, 130, 143-146
PROVINCES AND TERRITORIES—
  British Columbia........93, 97, 108, 119, 120, 121, 130, 131
  Keewatin 34, 92, 101
  Manitoba.......92, 97, 101, 107, 114, 119, 125, 130, 131, 139
  New Brunswick..............22, 26, 42, 47, 63, 73, 90,
                                 93, 101, 105, 119, 130
  Newfoundland..........................20, 21, 22, 88
  Nova Scotia.............22, 23, 26, 33, 35, 42, 47, 63.
                               73, 80, 93, 101, 119, 130, 132
  North-West 92, 107, 124, 131, 139
  Ontario 42, 46, 51, 93, 99, 101, 107, 112, 120
  Prince Edward Island 91, 100
  Quebec 48, 93, 104, 107, 110, 112, 118,
                               119, 121-124, 128, 130, 131

RAILWAYS....................80, 81, 87, 95, 97, 100-105,
                                 109, 115, 118, 121

TOPICAL INDEX. 159

REBELLIONS—
  Canadian 71-77
  Red River 97, 114
  North-West....................................... 114-118

SEIGNIORS 34, 45, 82
SLAVERY... 49, 53
STEAMBOATS 50, 68
TARIFFS (Legislation)............ 95, 102, 103, 104, 107, 121, 125,
                            126, 133, 134, 137, 139
TENURES (of Land)—
  Feudal 45
  Freehold 45
  Leasehold 91
  Seigniorial 45, 82
TREATIES—
  Aix-la-Chapelle................................... 36, 91
  Ashburton 79, 91
  Breda... 89
  France (Treaty with) 133, 141
  Ghent 63
  Indian 33, 101, 116
  Paris 38
  Reciprocity............................. 82, 87, 90, 126
  Ryswick 33, 88
  St. Germain-en-Laye 26, 89, 92
  Utrecht 33
  Versailles 41
  Washington 98, 102, 119, 122

UNITED EMPIRE LOYALISTS................... 40, 42, 51, 90, 91
UNITED STATES 27, 40, 41, 55-63, 70, 75, 79, 85, 86, 90, 98,
          101, 113, 116, 119, 122, 125, 126, 130, 133, 135
VETO POWER 100, 104, 103, 124, 125, 134, 143

www.ingramcontent.com/pod-product-compliance
Lightning Source LLC
Chambersburg PA
CBHW030317170426
43202CB00009B/1032